Home Is Where Your Clothes Are

A Comedy in two acts

Anthony Marriott and Bob Grant

Samuel French - London
New York - Toronto - Hollywood

First presented at the Theatre Royal, Stoke-on-Trent, Staffordshire, by David Tudor for Mayville Productions Ltd with the following cast:

Jill Palmer	Carolyn Jones
Major Alan Buxton	Philip Madoc
Postman	Adrian Bull
Philip Clarke	James Aidan
Ronald Chelmsford-Smythe	Richard Ratcliffe
Elizabeth Chelmsford-Smythe	Heather Chasen
Humphrey Bennett QC	Gordon Whiting
Brenda Bennett	Lyndsay Richardson
Jacqueline	Nikki Critcher

Directed by **Kim Grant**
Designed by **Michael Joyce**

CHARACTERS

Jill Palmer
Major Alan Buxton
Philip Clarke
Ronald Chelmsford-Smythe
Elizabeth Chelmsford-Smythe
Humphrey Bennett QC
Brenda Bennett
Jacqueline

The action takes place in the garden flat of a Victorian villa in Lancaster Gate, London

ACT I
   SCENE 1   9 o'clock Monday morning
   SCENE 2   5 o'clock Monday evening

ACT II   The same evening
Time—the present

ACT I

SCENE 1

The garden flat of a Victorian villa in Lancaster Gate, London. 9 o'clock Monday morning

The flat is comfortable, but not luxurious. DL is a walk-in wardrobe cupboard. Above it a single divan-bed, on which is a large teddy bear. UL is a door leading to the rest of the house. In the corner above it is an electricity meter and mains switch. In the upstage wall is a window, through which can be seen a small brick area, with steps going up to the street. UC is the front door to the area. To the right of the door is a small chest with three drawers, and to the right of that a pay-phone on the wall. On the wall R is a door, upstage, leading to the bathroom. DL is another door to the kitchen. The only other furniture is a small easy chair and a bedside table. There is a small suitcase on the easy chair

When the CURTAIN rises, Jill Palmer, late twenties, attractive and smartly dressed for the office, is tidying the bed. She goes to the cupboard and takes out a dress, which she puts in the suitcase. The case has several labels on it, Brussels, Paris, etc.

She goes into the kitchen and comes back with an empty milk bottle, picks up the case, her handbag and her car keys and goes out of the front door, shutting it behind her

After a moment there is a knock on the door UL. Major Alan Buxton, fifty, enters. He wears a sports jacket with leather patches on the elbows (which he wears over a cardigan) and cavalry twill trousers. The doorbell upstairs rings. The Major goes out of the front door

Postman (*off, at the top of the steps*) Morning, Major. Only two recorded deliveries this morning.

The Major goes up the steps

Major Ah, the War Office no doubt.
Postman (*off*) No sir, Inland Revenue and rates summons. I can spot them a mile off.
Major There must be some mistake.
Postman (*off*) Whatever you say Major. Sign here.

The Major comes back, carrying a sheaf of mail, all bills and demands. He quickly looks through them and is appalled. He goes to the kitchen door, knocks on it, and looks in. He repeats the same business at the bathroom door. Satisfied that there is no-one in the flat, he opens one of the letters, reads it and reacts in horror. He quickly goes to the phone and dials a number. After a moment he inserts a ten p piece

Major Hallo? National United Bank? ... Could I speak to the Manager please? ... Major Alan Buxton. ... What? He's expecting a call from me? ... Thank you. ... Hallo George, Alan here. Bit shocked by your letter. You didn't mean it did you? ... You did? ... Head Office? ... Did they really? ... Out of your hands? Oh my God! ... But that's my whole month's pension. What about next month's? ... You're going to swallow that up as well? ... Every month until it's paid off? At that rate I shan't be in credit till next year. What am I going to live on? ... But how am I going to pay all these bills if I can't cash any cheques? ... I know that's my problem, George, but I thought you could help me out. You gave me that impression when I took you out to lunch the other day—— What? You're not going to meet that cheque either? ... But you said how much you enjoyed your oysters—and the Dom Perignon—and the Château-briand.... Yes I know a man in my position shouldn't be buying expensive lunches, but you accepted my invitation.... I've told you before, I haven't got any security, she took practically all the furniture and it's her house and she won't sell it. And she expects me to pay all the bills and rent on top ... I have let the basement flat, as you suggested.... Yes, and roughing it upstairs in a sleeping bag.... I am trying to get a job, I've been trying for eighteen months, but there's not a lot of demand for a chap like me—retired regular—ex-infantry major—no qualifications and a Victoria Cross.... Blast, I haven't got another ten p.... George ... Mr Perkins ... Sir ... please ... (*The phone goes dead and he replaces the receiver*) Oh my God.

He looks at his watch, realizes that he has very little time and crosses to the bed, picks up the large teddy bear and throws it out of the door UL. *He then goes to the wardrobe, grabs all the dresses, shuts the wardrobe door and goes off* UL

Jill returns down the area steps with a bottle of milk. She goes into the kitchen, putting the car keys on the chair as she goes

The Major enters carrying a man's clothes, all on hangers, and puts them in the wardrobe. He goes to the chest of drawers and pulls one drawer open

Jill comes in from the kitchen

Jill Oh, Major!

The Major shuts the drawer quickly

Major Ah, Miss Palmer. I thought you'd gone.
Jill What are you doing in my flat?
Major I just popped down to use your phone.
Jill But you've got your own phone upstairs, in the house.
Major It's cut off ... cut out ... out of order. (*He quickly scrabbles up the bills from the chest and stuffs them in his pocket*)
Jill What are you doing with my furniture?

Major Er, it's the drawer. It sticks. I've been meaning to fix it.

Jill But there's nothing wrong with it.

Major Ah, that's right. I must have fixed it. I remember now, I did it a couple of weeks ago, before you moved in. Won't you miss your plane?

Jill No, I'm getting a later one.

Major Later? How much later?

Jill The ten-thirty. I've got plenty of time.

Major Are you going to do this every Monday morning?

Jill Do what?

Major Get the later plane?

Jill Does it matter?

Major No, no, of course not.

Jill Blast! I've forgotten to pack my evening bag. Where did I put it? Ah yes, the wardrobe.

Major The wardrobe. No! I mean, I'm sure you didn't.

Jill How would you know?

Major I wouldn't. I mean I wouldn't think I would, would you?

The kettle whistles in the kitchen

Your kettle's whistling.

Jill (*slightly puzzled*) Yes, it's a whistling kettle.

She goes into the kitchen

As soon as she has gone, the Major quickly whips the man's clothes out of the wardrobe and rushes out UL

Jill enters

Would you like a cup of . . . oh, he's gone.

She goes back to the kitchen

The Major enters carrying Jill's clothes, which he hastily returns to the wardrobe and closes the door. He then quickly gets the teddy bear from UL *and comes back as . . .*

Jill enters with a mug of coffee

The Major hastily hides the teddy behind his back

Oh, I thought you'd gone.

She turns away and puts her coffee cup down. He drops the teddy on the bed

Major Yes I had. I went upstairs . . . and then I came down again.

Jill Coffee?

Major No, clothes.

Jill Clothes?

Major And coffee. I spilt some coffee on my clothes. (*He brushes his sleeve, and sees the time on his watch*) Good God look at the time. I must get moving.

Jill Well don't let me keep you.

Major I'm not going anywhere. It's you. I mean you mustn't miss your plane. They need you in Brussels.
Jill Not really, I'm only a secretary.
Major But you're French-speaking. Mustn't keep the Frogs waiting.
Jill I'm sure the Common Market can survive for a few hours without me. My boss has got me till the end of the week.
Major Which day are you coming back?
Jill Friday evening, as usual.
Major That's all right then.
Jill If I had my way I wouldn't be going at all.
Major What?
Jill I hate Brussels. All my friends are in London. I've half a mind to chuck the job.
Major (*thoroughly alarmed*) Chuck it? You can't do that. It would ruin me. I mean it would ruin you. Think of all those people out of work. They're unemployed you know. Like me.
Jill It's different for you, you don't *have* to work.
Major Don't I? No I don't, do I.
Jill It must be nice to have a private income on top of your army pension.
Major Yes it must. I mean it is.
Jill Well I suppose I'd better be going.
Major Don't forget your case.
Jill It's in the car.
Major Oh, just one thing. The rent.
Jill What about it?
Major I wonder if I could trouble you for it?
Jill But it's not due for a fortnight.
Major Yes. I meant could I trouble you for it—in a fortnight.
Jill Well, yes, of course.
Major Good! I'll leave you to it.

He goes out UL

Jill (*as she goes*) Bye, see you Friday.

She shuts the door UL *and drops the latch on the Yale lock. She then goes out of the front door, closes it behind her, and goes up the area steps*

We hear a key going into the lock of the UL *door. The door opens and the Major appears holding a key. He dashes to the chest of drawers and opens a drawer*

Jill runs back down the steps and into the room

Forgot my evening bag.

She goes to the wardrobe and collects her evening bag

The Major slams the drawer on his hand

Major Ahh!! (*He hops around waving it*)
Jill Pardon?

Major Ah . . . you're back. I was just coming out to tell you, you didn't shut
the door properly.
Jill I thought I did.
Major No, it's a very tricky lock. I must fix it. After all you want your
privacy don't you. See you Friday. (*He starts to go*)
Jill That's funny. Teddy's moved.
Major He can't have done.
Jill I always sit him up on the pillow. It's nice and comfy for him.
Major I'll remember that. I mean I remember that.

*She puts her evening bag on the bed and arranges Teddy in his place. The
Major looks out of the window from time to time, and is rather agitated
throughout the following conversation*

Jill I meant to ask you—chest of drawers.
Major Chest of drawers?
Jill Could I have the other one back?
Major What other one?
Jill The matching one to that one. (*She indicates the chest*) The one you
took away to have repaired last week.
Major That one. Er . . . It fell apart.
Jill Fell apart? It was brand new.
Major Shoddy workmanship and full of woodworm.
Jill Just as well you got rid of it.
Major Exactly. (*He starts to go again*)
Jill But I do need another. I'm very short of drawer space.
Major You are? Of course you are.
Jill I'm sure you've got something upstairs I could have. Anything will do.
Major Anything? That's just it, I haven't got anything. Ex-wife left me very
short of furniture.
Jill How awkward for you. Couldn't you stop her?
Major Not really. It was her furniture.
Jill She can't do that.
Major But she did. I didn't want to make a fuss at eight o'clock in the
morning with the pantechnicon outside. Embarrassing enough as it was.
Jill At least she left you the house.
Major (*little chuckle*) Couldn't very well get that into the van.
Jill But you can't live with hardly any furniture.
Major Haven't got much option.
Jill Couldn't you order some more?
Major Yes, I could if I could find the . . . (*He stops in mid-sentence*)
Jill Find the what?
Major Find the sort of furniture I like.
Jill What sort do you like?
Major The sort my wife took away. It was antique. Worth a small fortune.
Jill That's why she took it.
Major Yes, I suppose it was.
Jill I didn't take a thing when I left my ex. I just packed a suitcase and left
him with the flat, the furniture and the little Maltese "scrubber" I found

him in bed with.

Major How very unpleasant for you. I know exactly how you feel—not that my adjutant was Maltese of course.

Jill You caught your wife in bed with the adjutant?

Major Good heavens no. It wasn't like that at all. I was the last to know.

Jill How did you find out?

Major She told me—the day I retired. We were watching *Panorama* at the time. She blurted it out. "You're leaving the Army and I'm leaving you." The pantechnicon was here in the morning.

Jill Didn't waste much time, did they?

Major No, they had it all planned. I'll say that for him, he was a damned good organizer. Best adjutant I ever had. There was nothing he couldn't turn his hand to.

Jill Including your wife it seems.

The Major looks at his watch, and once again out of the window

Are you expecting somebody?

Major Matter of fact I am. (*He doesn't move*)

Jill Don't let me keep you.

Major Don't let me keep you either.

Jill I ought to be going.

Major Off you go then.

Jill I will when you've gone.

Major Gone?

Jill Upstairs. To meet whoever it is you're going to meet.

Major Of course I've got to meet them upstairs haven't I. Have a nice trip— see you on Friday. It won't be *before* Friday evening will it?

Jill (*puzzled*) Course not. Never is, is it?

Major (*relieved*) Good.

Jill Good?

Major Good . . . goodbye.

He goes out UL. *Still puzzled, Jill shuts the door behind him and puts the Yale catch on, locking it. She then goes out of the front door, making sure that it is properly shut, and goes off up the area steps. We hear the car door slam and the car engine start*

The Major starts to rattle the UL *door violently. He cannot open it*

Major (*off*) Blast!

Jill comes running down the area steps, in through the front door, grabs her evening bag from the bed

The phone rings. She answers it

Jill Hallo? . . . Yes, speaking. . . . Oh I am sorry. . . . That is kind of you. It'll be lovely to have the week off. I do hope you get better soon, M'sieur Laugenie. Au'voir. (*She dials a number. Then puts a coin in the box*) Hallo, Paul? . . . Yes it's me, Jill. Can I take you up on your invitation? . . . Yes, I've got the week off. My boss has been taken ill. . . . Yes I should be able to make Highgate by half-past ten. I've just got a bit of shopping to do first and get changed. . . . Course I know the way. See you.

She puts the receiver down and goes out of the front door. We hear her drive off

Immediately the Major runs down the area steps, carrying two large plastic dustbin bags, one pink and one blue. He produces a door key and lets himself in. He takes out of the blue bag a pair of boxing gloves. He takes off the chest of drawers a can of hair lacquer and one or two toiletries, which he puts into the pink bag. He leaves the bags on the floor and goes to the cupboard, takes out the clothes and goes out UL

He returns immediately with a duvet, pillow and pair of men's pyjamas. He takes Teddy off the bed and plonks him in a chair. He then strips the pretty flowered duvet and matching pillow off the bed and the neatly folded night-dress, which he puts inside the zippered Teddy. He substitutes the striped duvet and matching pillow and pyjamas. He takes the rejected bedding out UL *and returns with three chest-drawers piled one on top of the other. He takes the three drawers out of the chest and substitutes the three he has just brought in. He goes out* UL *with the other drawers and returns with the man's clothes, which he hangs in the cupboard*

We hear a high-powered motor bike approaching

The Major reacts and hurriedly picks up both plastic bags and races into the bathroom. We hear him opening cupboards, etc. He reappears

The motor bike stops outside

The Major frantically dashes into the kitchen. Again we hear banging and crashing. He comes rushing out, still carrying both bags

At that moment Philip Clarke comes down the area steps. He is in his late twenties and a keen athlete. He is dressed in motor-cycling gear, crash helmet, etc. He lets himself in with a key

The Major suddenly notices Teddy in the chair, and picks him up and puts him on the bed as Philip, carrying a small valise, enters

Philip Morning, Major. What are you doing in my flat?
Major Ah, Mr Clarke. Just giving your flat a quick clean-up.
Philip That's very nice of you, but you needn't have bothered. I didn't leave it untidy when I left on Friday, did I?
Major No, no, spotless as usual. Everything's in order. Clothes wardrobe. Shirts in the drawers, Teddy on the bed. Oh!
Philip What's that doing there? That's not mine.
Major No . . . it's mine.
Philip Yours?
Major Yes.
Philip What are you doing with a teddy bear? Bit old for that kind of thing, aren't you?
Major Oh far too old. Gave up teddies years ago.

Philip Where did it come from?

Major Er ... I won it. The Conservative Club raffle. I was just wondering what to do with it. I ... er ... I'll give it away to somebody.

Philip If you're giving it away, my fiancée would love it. Brenda loves toys. Very kind of you.

Major (*weakly*) Don't mention it.

Philip (*about to take the teddy*) Can you just put it on the bed? My hands are covered in grease. Wretched bike broke down on the motorway. Belting down with rain. Got water on my plugs. And got soaked myself. I'd better have a shower and change before I go to chambers. The head man's a bit of a Tartar.

Major Yes. I've cleared the bathroom.

Philip How do you mean cleared it?

Major The drains. Had a bit of trouble with them over the weekend. But they're all right now.

Philip Good. (*He starts to take off his leathers. He wears a black jacket and pinstripe trousers underneath*)

Major Did you have a nice weekend?

Philip Very successful. I had a splendid fight.

Major Good gracious me. Do you like fighting?

Philip Naturally I do. I'm a keen amateur boxer.

Major Of course, the boxing gloves. I should have realized when I moved them.

Philip You moved them?

Major Yes, I picked them up, to look at them because ... I'm interested in boxing too.

Philip Really?

Major Did a lot of it in the army. Called me Battling Buxton.

Philip We must have a sparring session sometime. (*He shapes up and shadow boxes*)

Major (*backing away*) I'm very rusty. It was years ago.

Philip Don't worry, I won't hit you too hard. Tell you what, there's a Tournament on at the Albert Hall next Friday evening. I've got a couple of tickets. Would you like to come?

Major Friday? Oh no, Friday evening is my busy evening. I have to change over the flat.

Philip Change over the flat.

Major Change over the bedding.

Philip Don't worry about that. I'll do it. Just give me the clean bedding and I'll do it myself.

Major Good gracious. You're not staying Friday night are you?

Philip That depends. If you're not coming I'll persuade Brenda to come with me, and then I might as well stay here for the night.

Major Don't persuade her. I'll come.

Philip Good. To be quite honest, Brenda's not all that keen—in fact she hates it, in spite of the fact that that's how we met.

Major She boxes too?

Philip Goodness, no. It was the Midlands Barristers Boxing Club finals.

Her father presented me with the cup. He's the head of my chambers you know. I was area champion last year.

Major Congratulations.

Philip Thank you. Brenda was there with her father. I was knocked out.

Major I thought you won.

Philip I did. I mean I was knocked out by Brenda, and now we're engaged.

Major Congratulations again. Pretty good ring-craft, if I may say so, marrying the boss's daughter.

Philip I'm not doing it for that reason. I love her.

Major Course you do, now. I loved Elizabeth—my ex-wife—when I met her. She was the boss's daughter too. Her father was my general. It didn't do me much good. I finished up as a retired major and my wife ran off with the adjutant.

Philip I'm sorry.

Major So am I. He was my best friend.

Philip Why didn't you thump him?

Major Couldn't do that—he was my brother officer. Not done.

Philip Nor is stealing another officer's wife.

Major Oh that's done quite a lot. Mind you, Elizabeth's been very decent about the whole thing. She's let me stay on in the house. It's all hers you know, left her by the general when he had his accident.

Philip What happened to him?

Major He was eaten by a crocodile.

Philip In Africa?

Major No, in London Zoo. He'd had too much brandy. Crocodile was drunk for a week.

Philip What a terrible story.

Major Yes, but I mustn't worry you with my problems, you've got your living to earn.

Philip I've only got a couple of briefs to read today. Attempted murder and multiple rape. Pretty boring. Still mustn't grumble. I'm very lucky to have got into such good chambers.

Major But you still like to go home for weekends, don't you?

Philip Yes I do, but I think it's going to have to stop—because Brenda doesn't like it.

Major You mustn't let it stop—I mean you mustn't let her stop you.

Philip She *is* my fiancée, and her father is my head of chambers.

Major You won't like London at the weekends—it's a terrible place, very noisy. It's full of people from abroad.

Philip But I'll have Brenda.

Major Not here you won't. I mean she wouldn't like it here. I'm sure she's used to better things. She wouldn't like a nasty little flat like this.

Philip We'll soon find out. She's coming over tonight to cook my supper.

Major I shall have to tell her about the fungus and the damp, the mice and rats and the cockroaches.

Philip You didn't tell *me* about them.

Major No. They only come out at the weekends, because there's nobody here and it's so quiet.

Philip But I thought you said it was noisy at the weekends.

Major It is. From the rats, the mice and the cockroaches clumping about.

Philip In that case, I think you've got a nerve.

Major A nerve?

Philip Yes, for charging me so much rent. The place is infested.

Major Only at the weekends—and you're not here then are you?

Philip I might be. I'll have to give it plenty of thought.

Major That's right, give it plenty of thought—endless thought. You don't want to do anything I'll ... I mean you'll regret.

Philip I'll tell you one thing I'm regretting.

Major What's that?

Philip Paying you so much rent for a vermin-infested flat. You'd better get somebody in at the weekend.

Major I've already got somebody in—that's the trouble. I mean I've got somebody coming in to see to the trouble. But it's going to cost a lot of money and I haven't got a lot of money, so could I have the rent?

Philip But I paid you a month's rent in advance last week when I moved in.

Major Yes I know, but I mean *next* month's rent.

Philip You can't have that now, it's not due for three weeks. Anyway I haven't got it till the next lot of fees. And if I don't get to work soon I won't even have them. I'll lose the few briefs I've got. (*He goes towards the bathroom*)

Major Yes, well I mustn't keep you. (*He goes towards the door* UL)

Philip (*indicating the plastic bags*) Don't forget the rubbish.

Major That's not rubbish, that's her ... her ... herbaceous plants for the garden. I must put them upstairs. (*He picks up the bags*)

Philip I should put them in the garden.

Major What a good idea.

He goes UL

Philip takes off his jacket and chucks it on the bed. He goes into the bathroom, switches on the light and shuts the door

We hear a motor car approach and stop outside

The Major rushes in UL, *looks off out of the window. His worst fears confirmed, he hastily shoves the motor-bike leathers under the bed, takes Philip's jacket off the chair and throws it into the kitchen. Stuffs the boxing gloves into one of the drawers and picks up the motor-cycle helmet as ...*

Jill lets herself in from the outside. She carries a plastic bag of groceries and her handbag

Jill (*surprised*) Major! What are you doing here?

Major It was an emergency. I had to come down.

Jill Emergency? I don't understand. Why're you here?

Major Why're I here? Why're ... wire ... there's trouble with the wiring.

Jill What wiring?

Major Electrical wiring, what else.

Jill What's the matter with it?

Major It's overloading.

Jill That's terrible—it could start a fire.

Major Could it? Yes it could, that's why I've come down. And that's why you must get out. In case there is a fire. Could be one any second.

Jill There's no time to lose.

The Major rushes to the front door and holds it open for her. She follows him, but instead of going out of the door, she switches off the main electricity switch, which is on the wall by the door

Major What are you doing?

Jill It's all right now, I've switched it off, at the mains. Your wiring can't overload now.

Philip (*off, from the bathroom*) Oi! What's going on?

Jill There's a man in my bathroom.

Major So there is.

He rushes to the bathroom door, which has started to open. He pulls it shut

Stay where you are. Don't come out.

Philip (*off*) The bloody light's gone off.

Major The bloody light's gone off.

Jill Of course it has. I switched it off.

Major Of course it has. She switched it off.

Jill What are you doing in my bathroom?

Philip (*off*) I can't see to shower.

Jill What do you mean you can't see to shower?

Major No he means he can't see *to* the shower, which he's seeing to because he's the plumber.

Jill I thought you said it was the wiring?

Major It is.

Jill Then why have you got a plumber?

Major That's just it. The water's got into the wiring. So I've got the plumber in to get the water out. When the water's out I'll get the plumber out and the electrician in to get the wiring out.

Jill That makes sense.

Major Does it? Thank goodness.

Philip (*off*) When are you going to put the light on? I can't see what I'm doing.

Jill You'd better open the door to give him some light—he can't see what he's doing.

Major Yes. (*He starts to open the door, then quickly slams it again*) I can't do that. He hasn't got any clothes on.

Jill Hasn't got any clothes on? What sort of a plumber is he?

Major A naked one, but he's a very neat worker. There's so much water in there he took his clothes off. He didn't want to get them wet.

Philip (*off*) What the hell's going on?

Jill You'd better let me have a word with him.

Major No you can't. He's very shy and very nude. (*To Philip*) Hang on, I'll be with you in a minute. (*To Jill*) You go into the kitchen and I'll get him dressed.

Jill Where are his clothes? I can't see them.

Major No they're under the bed.

Jill Under the bed?

Major Yes I told him not to litter the place. He's very untidy.

Jill But you said he was a very neat worker.

Major Yes, he's a very neat worker, but a very untidy undresser. So you go in there and wait till I call you.

Jill Oh, very well, but don't be long.

She goes into the kitchen

Major Don't worry. I'll have him dressed in a flash. (*He closes the kitchen door behind her*)

Philip, with a bath towel round his waist, comes out of the bathroom

Philip What's going on and what are you doing in my flat?

Major It's an emergency. It's the wiring and the water. There's water in the wiring, but don't worry, I've had the electrician in and he's fixed it. He's a very good man. I'll put the electricity back on. (*He goes to the main electricity switch and switches it on*)

Jill (*off*) Is he dressed yet?

Philip There's a girl in my kitchen.

Major So there is.

Philip What's she doing there and who is she?

Major She's . . . the electrician.

Philip You said the electrician was a man.

Major Yes he is, but she's . . . the electrician's mate. His wife. She checks up on him, he's very sloppy.

Philip I thought you said he was a very *good* man?

Major Oh he is, he's a very good *man*, but a very sloppy *worker*.

Jill (*off*) Hurry up, I want to speak to the plumber.

Philip What plumber?

Major She means you . . . you don't know what she means. She means Mr Plummer, the electrician, that's his name. And she's Mrs Plummer. (*He calls off to the kitchen*) Won't be a minute Miss Palmer.

Philip Why are you calling her Miss Palmer?

Major Because that's her name, her maiden name, before she married Mr Plummer and became Mrs Plummer.

Jill (*off*) Hurry up, I haven't got all day.

Philip You'd better let me have a word with her. (*He goes towards the kitchen door*)

Major No, you can't do that, you haven't got any clothes on. She mustn't see you like that.

Philip I'm perfectly decent, I'm sure she won't mind.

Major No, *she* won't mind, but her husband will. He's insanely jealous. He gets very violent.

Philip (*shaping up*) Don't worry. I can handle myself.

Major No, you mustn't hit him, he's . . . he's not well, he's got a weak heart.

Philip A weak heart?

Major Yes, you wouldn't want his death on your conscience or on your carpet, would you?

Jill (*off*) Do get a move on.

Major Yes, do get a move on ... and have your shower, so that she can come out and check the wiring.

Philip I hope this isn't going to happen very often. (*He goes to the bathroom door*)

Major So do I!

The kitchen door starts to open

Quick! (*He bundles Philip off into the bathroom*)

Philip exits into the bathroom

The Major shuts the door

Jill, carrying Philip's black jacket, enters from the kitchen

Jill Where's the plumber?

Major He's gone. I've sent him away.

Jill Without his jacket? (*She holds it up*)

Major Well I told you he was an untidy undresser, he's an untidy *dresser* as well.

Jill (*crossing to the bed*) Well I suppose he'll come back for it. (*She puts the jacket on the bed, feels something with her foot, bends down and pulls out the leathers*) He must be untidy, he can't be dressed at all.

Major No, they're not the plumber's clothes, they belong to ... er ... to someone else ... er ... to the previous tenant. He must have forgotten them.

Jill Why did he keep dirty leather clothes under the bed?

Major Ah, that's just it. He *was* dirty, very dirty. Dirty-minded, that's why I had to get rid of him.

Jill I should think so.

Major Yes, *he* was bad enough, but you should have seen the people he brought back here.

Jill He sounds very unsavoury. I wouldn't like to meet him.

Major Don't worry, I'll make sure you don't. Hadn't you better go?

Jill I don't want to go yet.

Major What do you mean? You'll miss your plane.

Jill But I'm not catching a plane.

Major Surely you're not going to Brussels by boat, you'll never get there. It's not on the coast.

Jill I don't want to get to Brussels. I'm not going.

Major What do you mean, not going?

Jill Well not this week anyway.

Major But you can't stay here, not during the week.

Jill Why ever not?

Major Well you never do. You don't know what it's like during the week. It gets very crowded here. It's full of people. I mean London's full of people.

Jill Yes, you're right. The traffic was terrible this morning. I had an awful job to find a space outside.

Major You haven't parked outside have you?

Jill Of course, I always do.

Major That's at weekends. You haven't got a permit—they'll tow you away, and this is their worst time for doing it. They're always here on the dot.

Jill The dot of what?

Major What time is it now?

Jill (*looking at her watch*) Nine twenty-five.

Major The dot of nine twenty-five. You must move your car at once, before it's too late.

Jill I'll have to risk it. Surely I'll be all right for a couple of minutes.

Major (*glancing at the bathroom*) Yes, I think you'll be all right provided they're very short minutes.

Jill Well, if you'll excuse me, I'll just get changed. (*She starts to go towards the cupboard*)

Major Yes of course. (*He realizes, and then rushes between her and the cupboard*) Of course *not*!

Jill Of course not what?

Major Of course you can't risk it.

Jill I suppose you couldn't do me a tremendous favour and park it for me, could you. (*She smiles sweetly and hands him her car keys from her handbag*)

Major (*looking at the bathroom door again*) I can't. I mustn't . . . drive.

Jill Mustn't drive.

Major I'm banned.

Jill What for?

Major Driving while I was disqualified.

Jill What am I going to do then?

Major I've just remembered. There are some new meters a couple of streets away. That should give me . . . that should take you ten minutes.

Jill I'd better do that then. Which street are they in?

Major I can't remember exactly, but if you drive around a few times you're bound to see them.

Jill That could take me hours.

Major Good . . .

Jill Good?

Major . . . ness me, no. I should hurry up though. They fill up very rapidly.

Jill If I must, I must, I suppose.

Major Yes, go quickly, but when you've gone go slowly. I mean watch your speed.

Jill goes out of the front door, up the area steps

Immediately the Major dashes to the cupboard and goes inside

At this moment, Jill comes down the area steps again, and comes into the flat

Jill (*as she enters*) Major, you haven't got . . . ? (*She sees he isn't there*)

The Major shoots out of the cupboard and closes the door behind him

What are you doing in my wardrobe?

Major I was just going to move the clothes.

Jill Move my clothes!?

Major No, not *your* clothes. *His* clothes.

Jill His clothes?

Major The previous tenant's. I thought he might have left some in there—as well as under the bed.

Jill There are no men's clothes in there. I know that.

Major I didn't—but I do now. I know exactly what's in there. You haven't parked your car already have you?

Jill Course not. I need some ten ps for the parking meter.

Major Is that all. (*He fishes in his pockets*) Here you are. (*He looks at his small change*) I haven't got any.

Jill No point in me moving the car then, is there?

Major But you must move it. Hold on, I've got an idea.

He dashes into the bathroom and reappears almost immediately with Philip's trousers. He takes out coins from a pocket

Here you are. Here's a couple. (*He gives them to her*)

Jill Whose are those trousers?

Major What? Er . . . the plumber's.

Jill I can't take the plumber's money.

Major Yes you can, I'll pay him back. (*He takes a pound coin out of his pocket*) Look a pound coin. (*He puts it into the trouser pocket*) Quick, off you go.

Jill runs out and up the area steps

The Major takes the pound out again as . . .

Philip, wearing his dressing-gown, comes out of the bathroom

Philip What's the idea, pinching my trousers. And you're pinching my money as well. (*He takes the trousers*)

Major No, I only took two ten ps out and I'm putting a pound back.

Philip You might have asked me first.

Major I hadn't time. It was urgent. For the meter.

Philip What meter?

Major What meter? Not what meter, slot meter. The gas meter. The gas was running out and I didn't want you have have a cold shower.

Philip But the gas isn't on a slot meter.

Major Isn't it? Ah, that's probably why I couldn't get the ten ps into it.

Philip Well you might as well take your pound back. (*He takes it out of the trouser pocket and gives it to the Major*)

Major Oh thank you very much.

Philip And I'll have my two ten ps back. (*He holds out his hand*)

Major Er . . . I haven't got them.

Philip (*surprised*) Why not?

Major Well I got rid of them. When they wouldn't go in the gas meter . . . I . . . er . . . (*he looks round*) . . . I put them in the phone box.

Philip Whatever for?

Major Er . . . I made a phone call. That's it. I phoned the Gas Board . . . to tell them to come and fit a slot meter. I thought it would be better.

Philip Well it would, but do we have to go into that now. I want to get dressed and go to chambers.

He looks at the Major expecting him to leave. The Major doesn't take the hint

Major Yes I would if I were you, as quickly as possible.

Philip If you wouldn't mind . . . ?

Major Mind what?

Philip Mind leaving, I want to get dressed.

Major Oh yes of course. (*He starts to go* UL) No! You can't get dressed in here!

Philip Why not? It's my flat. (*He starts to get clean clothes from the chest and cupboard*)

Major She might see you. She'll be here any minute. She's only just parking her car.

Philip She?

Major The girl . . . I mean the old girl who comes here to clean. She's very easily shocked. She's led a sheltered life. She's terrified of men. She was a nun. You'd better dress in the bathroom.

Philip Well tell her to start by cleaning the bathroom and I'll dress here.

Major I can't *tell* her what to do. She won't take orders from me, she wouldn't even take the Holy Orders orders. That's why she was asked to leave the convent.

Philip She sounds a very difficult lady.

Major She is, she's impossible. But I can't afford to lose her. That's why you must go into the bathroom.

Philip Oh all right. I'll only be two minutes.

Major Two minutes? I can't move this lot in two minutes.

Philip Move what?

Major Er . . . the furniture. She insists I move all the furniture out so that she can clean behind it. She's very thorough. They taught her in the convent "Cleanliness is next to Godliness".

Philip There's absolutely no necessity to move everything out.

Major Oh there is. If I don't, she'll find out and she'll leave. And she's a very good tenant.

Philip Tenant? I thought she was the cleaning lady?

Major She is *and* she's a tenant. Upstairs. She lives in the attic. She had nowhere to go when they threw her out of the convent, so I let her have the attic. Hurry up and go in there. (*Indicating the bathroom*) She'll be back any second.

Philip I'll be as quick as I can.

Major No I mean hurry up and *go* in there, but don't hurry up *in* there. I mean you want to look your best.

Philip Yes, my head of chambers expects you to be smart, even if you're not appearing in court.

He goes into the bathroom with his clothes

The Major goes to the cupboard, takes out Philip's clothes and goes off UL *accidentally dropping a tie near the cupboard*

Philip comes out of the bathroom, still in his dressing-gown, goes to the cupboard, stops with his hand on the knob, sees the tie on the floor, picks it up

Ah that's the one, must have dropped it.

He goes back into the bathroom and shuts the door, just as . . .

The Major struggles on UL *carrying two drawers, with Jill's clothes from the cupboard draped over the top. He puts the drawers down, hangs her clothes in the cupboard, then removes the bottom two drawers from the chest and replaces them with the drawers containing Jill's clothes. He then takes Philip's two drawers off* UL

Philip comes out of the bathroom, now wearing his trousers and carrying his dressing-gown, which he hangs on the hook on the back of the door UL*. He then goes to the chest, opens the top drawer, takes out a pair of socks, leaves the drawer open and goes out to the bathroom*

The Major returns carrying the third drawer of Jill's clothes. He reacts to the open drawer and looks towards the bathroom, puzzled. He changes over the top drawers and then goes to the door UL *with Philip's drawer. He sees Philip's dressing-gown hanging on the back of the door. He tucks the drawer under his arm, collects the dressing-gown and goes off, shutting the door behind him*

Jill comes down the area steps, carrying her case, and lets herself into the flat. She goes to the cupboard and takes out casual clothes. She is starting to to undress when . . .

The Major comes in carrying her négligé

Major Ah!
Jill Oh! You could've knocked.
Major I didn't know you were back.
Jill What are you doing with my négligé?
Major Good gracious, is this yours? I never realized this was yours. I thought it belonged to the other one.
Jill You mean the previous tenant?
Major Exactly.
Jill He didn't have a négligé did he?
Major Yes he did. I told you before he was kinky. That's why I got rid of him.
Jill Well it's not his, it's mine. And it was very expensive. Brand new, I haven't worn it yet.

Major I'm glad it's yours. I shan't have to take it back to him. (*He hangs the négligé on the* UL *door*)

Jill I hope you're going to take these leather things back to him. (*She indicates the leathers on the floor*)

Major (*gathering them up*) Yes, I will.

Jill If you'll excuse me I want to get changed.

Major Yes . . . no. Not in here.

Jill Why ever not, it's my flat.

Major Yes it is, but the plumber's coming back.

Jill That's all right, he'll be in the bathroom.

Major He already is . . . I mean he's already been in there and found that the fault is in here. It's pipes under the floor. He's got to dig it all up.

Jill If that's the case, I'm glad I'm going away for a few days.

Major So am I.

Jill I'll go and change in the bathroom. (*She picks up her clothes, and goes towards the bathroom*)

Major You can't, it's full up.

Jill Full up?

Major With water. It's turning out to be much worse than I thought. You'd better go into the kitchen.

Jill I suppose I'll have to. It's very inconvenient for me.

Major It is for me too. I mean it's rather inconvenient all round.

Jill If they're going to dig up the floor, I'd better move my clothes. I don't want them getting dirty.

Major I'll do it. Let me do it. I was going to do it anyway.

Jill That's very kind of you. The easiest thing to do will be just to take the drawers out of the chest.

Major It is. I mean it is a good idea. Have you got everything you want out of them?

Jill Yes, thank you.

Major Then I'll do it right away.

Jill goes to the kitchen, taking her clothes with her

The Major takes the drawers out, and takes them off UL

Philip comes out of the bathroom, now fully dressed. He goes to the chest of drawers and reacts

The Major returns, carrying three drawers (Philip's)

Philip What are you doing with my drawers?

Major Your drawers? Yes these are your drawers.

Philip Where have you been with them?

Major I took them out because the plumber's coming to dig up the floor, and I didn't want your things to get dirty.

Philip What are you bringing them back for?

Major I thought you might want something out of them.

Philip Yes I do, as a matter of fact, I want a handkerchief.

Major Help yourself.

Philip takes a handkerchief out of the top drawer

Philip Thanks. You can take them out now.
Major Thank you. I expect you'll be wanting to get to work now.

He takes the drawers out UL *and returns immediately*

Philip Yes I do. But I've got a couple of phone calls to make first. I shouldn't be more than half an hour.
Major Half an hour!
Philip Yes. I'm in no rush. I'm going to make myself a cup of coffee first. (*He starts towards the kitchen*)
Major No you can't.
Philip Yes I can. I'm perfectly capable of making myself a cup of coffee.
Major Not without water you're not, and there isn't any. The plumber's had to turn it off.
Philip That's all right. I'll have a glass of milk instead.
Major You can't, it's off. You know the electricity went off. So the fridge went off and then the milk went off. And it's time you went off.
Philip Yes, as soon as I've done my paperwork.
Major There's no time for that. I've just remembered, there was a phone call for you.
Philip Why didn't you tell me before?
Major I couldn't. I hadn't thought of it before. I mean, I'd forgotten it until now. And now I've remembered. Your boss wants to see you in chambers now.
Philip Now?
Major Yes. It was now then. So it's past now, now.
Philip Humphrey Bennett wants to see me?
Major He didn't give his name.
Philip How do you know it was him then?
Major It sounded like him, and anyway he mentioned the name of your fiancée.
Philip He mentioned Brenda?
Major Is that her name? Yes, he mentioned her several times.
Philip He wants to see me about Brenda?
Major Yes, that's what he wants to see you about.
Philip Oh dear, I hope there hasn't been any trouble.
Major Yes there has, lots of it. He kept on saying Brenda and trouble and you.
Philip Do you mean Brenda's in trouble?
Major You should know. Have you . . . ?
Philip Yes.
Major Well, there you are then. That's what it's about. I should get there as quickly as possible, if I were you.
Philip You're right. This is terrible. What am I going to say?
Major You'll think of something. I always do. I find it's amazing the things you come out with when the pressure's on. I think the pressure's on you, old chap.

Philip I knew I should never have given in to her.

Major I don't think her father'll see it that way. As he said, she's his only daughter.

Philip She's got four sisters.

Major But she's the only daughter he's got in this condition. That's what he said. He's hopping mad.

Philip I don't think I can face him.

Major You must. You must go, because she'll be out of the kitchen in a minute.

Philip Brenda's in the kitchen?

Major (*realizing his mistake*) I mean she's in the kitchen at home. He's banished her there. Then he's going to throw her out, when he goes home.

Philip I must stop him. He's a terrible man when he's roused. I hope he doesn't make me hit him.

He goes off up the area steps

Jill enters from the kitchen. She has changed her outfit and carries her other clothes

Jill Who was that?

Major Er . . . that was the plumber. He's just finished.

Jill You mean he's dug up the floor, mended the pipes, put the floor back again and relaid the carpet all in two minutes. That's impossible.

Major Yes it is. That's why it was lucky he didn't have to do any of that. It was all a mistake, it was the house next door

Jill He looked very smart for a plumber. Black jacket and pinstripes.

Major He's very eccentric—delusions of grandeur. But he's a very good plumber. That's why he realized right away the problem wasn't here, but next door.

Jill That's a relief. Perhaps you'd be kind enough to bring my things back.

Major Yes of course. Delighted.

He goes out UL

Jill hangs her suit up in the cupboard and comes back into the room

The phone rings. She answers it

Jill Hallo? . . . Who? . . . Sorry Brenda, there's no Philip living here. You must have the wrong number. . . . Yes, that's my number, but I assure you no-one called Philip lives here.

The Major enters with Jill's drawers

(*Into the phone*) Hang on. Major, there's someone called Brenda who insists there's a Philip living here. Do you know anything about it?

Major (*alarmed*) Philip? Yes, he was the previous tenant, the one I told you about.

Jill Oh him. (*Into the phone*) I'm sorry Brenda, but the Major's had to turf your kinky boyfriend out. . . . Oh hasn't he told you about that? Oh yes, he's been slung out, leather gear, female clothes and all. . . . Well, if you don't believe me you can ask the Major yourself. Here he is.

She hands the receiver to the Major, who takes it with great reluctance

Major Oh ... er ... hallo, Brenda. ... No we haven't met. ... Philip. ... Yes. ... No, of course I haven't, but he's not here *now*. He's gone to your father. ... I think it's something rather personal. ... Yes, I should ring him there if I were you. Goodbye, Brenda. (*He puts the receiver down*)

Jill She seems to think that Philip still lives here.

Major He obviously hasn't told her. I think he's trying to get rid of her. You see he's got her pregnant.

Jill Really?

Major Yes. The trouble is, he works for her father.

Jill What sort of man's *he*?

Major I don't know. I've never spoken to him. But he sounds pretty unpleasant.

Jill Just the sort of person this Philip deserves if you ask me. Anyway, they're not your worry. I'm sure you won't see Philip again.

Major Not till six o'clock ... er, when I take his leathers back to him.

Jill Does he live near here then?

Major A bit too close for comfort.

Jill Well I hope I never meet him.

Major So do I.

Jill I'm going to be awfully late for my feller. Not that it matters.

She puts her suitcase on the bed, opens it and takes out a dress. During the following she swaps the dress for another from the cupboard

Major Is he an old friend?

Jill No, I've only met him once. At a party on Saturday. Something to do with the music business I think.

Major Still, it's nice of his family to invite you.

Jill Oh he doesn't live with his family. He's got a studio flat on his own in Highgate.

Major But where will you sleep?

Jill Well with him of course.

Major But you don't even know anything about him.

Jill That's why I'm going to sleep with him. I shall know a lot more about him by the end of the week.

Major Good gracious! You can't be sure you love him after only one meeting.

Jill Course I don't love him. What's love got to do with it?

Major Well, everything I should have thought.

Jill You *are* old-fashioned.

Major Yes I think I must be. Sorry.

Jill Don't be. It's rather refreshing. I only wish I were like you. But after my divorce, I decided it was safer to play the field. That way you don't get emotionally involved.

Major You must have been very hurt by your divorce.

Jill Well I was a bit upset at the time, but it was a relief to get rid of him.

Major Still I expect it's left its mark. These things do. I still miss Elizabeth.

And Ronald, too, come to that.

Jill Ronald?

Major The adjutant.

Jill But they treated you shamefully.

Major Yes I suppose they did. But it's still a wrench when you lose your wife and your best friend on the same day.

Jill You should get out more, meet new people. Live it up a bit, like me.

Major I'm a bit old for that sort of thing. Anyway, I don't know any young ladies in Highgate.

Jill Don't be silly, you're not old, you're in the prime of life.

Major I'm also out of work and rather broke.

Jill Tell you what, when I get back from Highgate, I'll take you out to supper, and we can cry on each other's shoulders.

Major I couldn't possibly let you take me out, it wouldn't be right.

Jill Well, you're like me, you're not attached.

Major No, I mean I couldn't let you pay.

Jill Why ever not? I'm a working girl and I earn very good money.

Major That's not the point. I just couldn't.

Jill I'll bet you're the sort of person who gives up his seat to old ladies on buses.

Major Doesn't everybody?

Jill Where have you been for the last twenty years?

Major In the army.

Jill That accounts for it. All right, you can pay if you insist.

Major I do, but funds are rather low at the moment.

Jill Don't worry, we'll sort it out between us, but we must definitely have an evening out together.

Major It's a very nice idea, Miss Palmer. I must say I really would enjoy it.

Jill We're not going to have a lot of fun if you're going to call me Miss Palmer all evening. My name's Jill, and you're . . .

Major Alan, actually.

Jill All right, Alan, it's a date then. We'll have a good old chat when I get back. (*She closes the suitcase*)

Major I hope you enjoy your . . . er . . . your visit to Highgate.

Jill Well I've said I'll go, so I might as well. I'll tell you all about it on Saturday.

Major Yes, well . . . er . . . as you please. Enjoy yourself anyway.

Jill picks up her handbag and the suitcase

Oh here, please allow me.

Jill There's no need.

Major I insist. (*He takes the suitcase from her*) I'm going out anyway. I thought I'd spend the day at the zoo. The chimpanzee's tea party reminds me of home.

Jill I'll drop you off, it's on my way.

Major Oh, thank you.

They start to go

Jill Do you know, Alan, the last person to carry my case for me was my father.

Major I suppose I am that old.

Jill I didn't mean it like that. You're years younger than Daddy.

Major I must say I feel a lot younger than I did.

He holds the door open for her. She goes out, followed by him. They go up the area steps together as——

——the CURTAIN *falls*

SCENE 2

It is five p.m. of the same day.

The door UL *opens and Ronald comes in, followed by Elizabeth. Ronald Chelmsford-Smythe is in his mid-thirties, good-looking, smartly dressed—a bit too smartly. He is every inch a con-man. Elizabeth Chelmsford-Smythe is in her mid-forties and strikingly good-looking. She is also very well dressed in the height of fashion. They both wear smart top coats. Elizabeth switches on the main lights*

Ronald My word, Elizabeth, there is a lot of it.

Elizabeth It's a big house, Ronald. We'll have a good look round after tea.

Ronald I don't think I'll bother with tea. They'll be open at five-thirty. That's only half an hour.

Elizabeth I would have thought you'd had enough at lunchtime.

Ronald That was just a few beers, now it's time for my pink gins. I suppose there isn't someone around to rustle one up, is there?

Elizabeth No there isn't. Of course when Daddy was alive we had servants. Still, Alan seems to have kept the place clean and tidy. Apart from all that junk outside. I'll have to get him to move that.

Ronald I suppose this is his little pad is it?

Elizabeth I couldn't very well chuck him out altogether. I mean you know the terms of Daddy's will as well as I do.

Ronald (*seeing the teddy bear on the bed*) Has he gone into his second childhood?

Elizabeth What do you mean?

Ronald (*pointing to the teddy*) That thing. That bear.

Elizabeth I've never seen that before. He never used to sleep with a teddy bear. Perhaps he's missing me.

Ronald He's obviously going a bit peculiar. It's not safe to leave him in the house, now he's going senile.

Elizabeth Nonsense. Anyway he does pay me rent.

Ronald That's a joke, he's two months behind. We could do with the money now. I noticed the phone upstairs isn't working. I suppose he hasn't paid that bill either.

Elizabeth Don't be silly, Ronald, Alan doesn't need the one upstairs, he's got the pay-phone down here.

Ronald Damned inconvenient. I'll have to pay cash for my calls. Just as well

I took the precaution of phoning your bank manager this morning from the airport.

Elizabeth What did you say to him?

Ronald I told him to sell more of your shares, of course.

Elizabeth There can't be many left.

Ronald There aren't. That was the last thousand.

Elizabeth Just as well you've got that job in Saudi Arabia.

Ronald It's all very well for you. You haven't got to go tinkering about with tractors in the desert.

Elizabeth You shouldn't have got yourself chucked out of the army, then you wouldn't have to.

Ronald That wasn't my fault. I only borrowed the money from the Regimental Account, I had every intention of paying it back.

Elizabeth Of course *I* know that, and *you* know that, but the Court Martial didn't know that.

Ronald What else was I to do? I was suddenly landed with a lot of extra expenses. Alan's got a hell of a lot to answer for, slinging you out of the house.

Elizabeth He didn't sling me out. I left him.

Ronald He let you go—that's the same thing isn't it. So naturally I felt obliged to do the decent thing and marry you.

Elizabeth Thanks very much. You said you loved me.

Ronald Love's one thing. Marriage is another. You didn't have to leave him.

Elizabeth I couldn't go on deceiving him any longer.

Ronald I could. I was flabbergasted when you turned up on the doorstep with your suitcase.

Elizabeth There's no need to go on about it. What else could I do?

Ronald You could've stayed with Alan.

Elizabeth Then I couldn't have been with you.

Ronald I could've looked you up when I came home on leave.

Elizabeth That's nice. What was I supposed to be, home comforts for the troops. "Make a soldier happy—he might be dead tomorrow."

Ronald It's done now. There's no further point in talking about it. I don't think I'll go to Saudi Arabia. I've gone off the whole idea.

Elizabeth You've got to go. They've bought us the tickets. We're going on that nine o'clock flight in the morning whether you like it or not. You're very lucky they're allowing me to come with you.

Ronald Are you sure you couldn't sell this house?

Elizabeth You know perfectly well I can't. Daddy only left it to me in Trust.

Ronald Stupid old fool. I always said he had no brains.

Elizabeth Don't you talk about Daddy like that. He was a full-blown general. You're only a cashiered captain.

Ronald No need to rub it in. I'm suffering enough as it is.

Elizabeth I'm not exactly enjoying this life myself. They've stopped my account at Harrods.

Ronald You should have paid it.

Elizabeth What with?

Ronald The money you got from Alan. What have you done with that?

Elizabeth You've spent it.

Ronald A chap's got to live. Got to have the basics.

Elizabeth The basics are not booze, betting and birds.

Ronald Birds? Now you're going too far.

Elizabeth Don't think I don't know about little Sandy from the NAAFI.

Ronald What about her? I thought everybody knew about her.

Elizabeth They knew about you as well. You're lucky she didn't name you as the father of her baby.

Ronald That's why I made the Post Corporal marry her—that's what she wanted.

Elizabeth What about the time I caught you with the Quartermaster's daughter in the stores.

Ronald She was helping me count blankets.

Elizabeth Funny way to count them from underneath. And the RSM's niece. You were for-ever pinching her bottom.

Ronald A chap's got to be sociable—she was half Italian. They like that sort of thing.

Elizabeth The way you were behaving, it was just as well you were cashiered.

Ronald That's hitting a fellow under the belt.

Elizabeth That's where you ought to be hit.

Ronald If you're going to attack me, I'm going off to the Infantry Club.

Elizabeth You're not a member.

Ronald Jack Featherstone is.

Elizabeth You're not meeting him are you?

Ronald Why not. Jolly decent fellow Jack. Going to let me in on one of his schemes. He says I'll make a fortune, then I won't have to go to Saudi Arabia.

Elizabeth The only person who'll make a fortune will be Jack Featherstone. Still there's one consolation, he can't get any more out of you—you haven't got any.

Ronald He doesn't want any money out of me, he wants my financial advice.

Elizabeth I should think you're the last person to ask.

Ronald I don't have to listen to any more of this. I'll see you later.

Elizabeth If you can still focus.

Ronald I shall need a spot of loose change for the taxi and so on.

Elizabeth looks in her purse

Elizabeth I've only got twenty pounds.

Ronald Is that all. I suppose that'll have to do. (*He takes the money and stuffs it in his pocket*)

Elizabeth Don't be late, we've got all our stuff to unpack.

Ronald Get Alan to give you a hand. He's good at that sort of thing. Cheers.

He goes out of the front door and up the area steps

Elizabeth gets a letter out of her handbag, looks at it, goes to the phone and dials a number. After a moment she puts a coin into the box

Elizabeth Hallo, is that Humphrey Bennett's Chambers? . . . Oh, Humphrey, it's you. . . . Elizabeth Chelmsford-Smythe. . . . Yes, I must have your private line. I got your letter. . . . Of course I'm not ringing from a call box in Kowloon. We're at home. Back in this country. . . . No, not on leave. Ronald isn't in the army any more. They had a bit of a disagreement. . . . Of course, you haven't met Ronald have you. Funny, you've never met either of my husbands. . . . Yes, we're in the house. . . . The flat? That's where I'm speaking from. . . . Well of course you can rent it if you want to. That's no problem. I had no idea you were looking for one. . . . Oh, I see, just for when you're working late in Town. . . . We'd be delighted to have you, Humphrey. . . . Well why don't you pop round now, we're off to the Middle East tomorrow. Then you can decide if you'd like to take it. . . . Well I thought about three hundred pounds a month. . . . Good, look forward to seeing you in about a quarter of an hour. *Ciao*, Humphrey.

She puts the phone down and looks around the flat to see if it needs tidying up. She picks up the teddy, examines it, sees the zip at the back, undoes it and pulls out Jill's very feminine night-dress. The phone rings, she drops the nightie on the bed, and still holding the teddy, goes to the phone and lifts the receiver

Hallo? . . . I beg your pardon? . . . Where the *what* am I? . . . There's no need to say that word again, I heard you the first time. . . . No this is not Jill speaking. . . . No I am not her flat mate. . . . I've no idea where she is, in fact I don't even know her. . . . You must have the wrong number. . . . I have no intention of coming to Highgate . . . and certainly not for that!

She slams the receiver down. Then she looks around the room, drops the teddy in the chair R and goes to the bathroom door, opens it, switches on the light and looks in. Satisfied, she closes the door and goes out to the kitchen, switching on the light

The Major comes down the area steps, jauntily, and lets himself into the flat, closing the door behind him. He is carrying a zoo catalogue. He goes to the chest and opens a drawer

Elizabeth enters from the kitchen

Elizabeth Ah, there you are.

The Major slams the drawer shut and spins round

Major Ah! Elizabeth! What on earth are you doing here?
Elizabeth We've come back.
Major We?
Elizabeth Ronald and I of course.
Major But six months ago he was posted to Hong Kong for two years. He can't be back already.
Elizabeth He's not in the army now.
Major Not in the army. But it was his whole life. Did he buy himself out?

Elizabeth It was to do with money, but not in that way. We had a bit of a problem. That's why we're back here.

Major What both of you?

Elizabeth Yes. But we're leaving for Saudi Arabia in the morning. Ronald's got a job out there.

Major That's all right then. Just a minute, where am I going to sleep tonight?

Elizabeth Down here, naturally, where you've been living all the time.

Major Oh yes of course, I have, haven't I.

Elizabeth By yourself.

Major By myself, naturally. There's no-one else down here. (*Anxiously*) You haven't seen anyone else down here, have you?

Elizabeth No.

Major That's all right then.

Elizabeth Only Teddy.

Major Teddy who?

Elizabeth (*pointing to the bear*) Teddy bear. That teddy.

Major Oh, that teddy. Dear old Teddy. Yes, there's just the two of us.

Elizabeth Which of you wears the nightie?

Major Nightie? I always wear pyjamas. You know I always wear pyjamas.

Elizabeth Then whose is this? (*She holds up the nightie*)

Major That must be ... er ...

Elizabeth Whose must that be?

Major Yes, I don't know whose that must be.

Elizabeth I found it inside Teddy.

Major Did you? I thought he'd lost weight.

Elizabeth What was it doing there?

Major I don't know what it was doing there. Yes I do. It must have been there all the time.

Elizabeth All what time?

Major You see, I won Teddy in a raffle. It was a second-hand raffle, so naturally Teddy was second-hand, and that night-dress must have belonged to the previous owner, who must have been a girl.

Elizabeth That's possible I suppose. As long as you're not bringing girls in here. I'm not having that kind of thing under my roof.

Major I wouldn't dream of it. You ... er, haven't found anything else, have you?

Elizabeth No, only those clothes outside the door there. (*She indicates the door* UL)

Major Oh those clothes. (*Anxiously, he can't remember which they are*) Er ... what *sort* of clothes are they?

Elizabeth Just clothes. I didn't notice anything unusual about them.

Major If there's nothing unusual about them, they're mine.

Elizabeth Perhaps you'd like to settle up the rent with me now. You're two months behind.

Major Things are a bit tight at the moment. You see I haven't got a job.

Elizabeth They're very tight for us too. So if you can't afford the rent, I'll just have to get someone in who can. It's easy enough to let this flat.

Major It was. I mean it always was a desirable little flat. I'm sure you'll have no trouble letting it.

Elizabeth I'm glad you appreciate that. I may want you to move. I must get down to the shops, I haven't got any food in. (*She closes the door* UL *without seeing the négligé on the back of the door*)

Major (*seeing it and reacting in horror*) Ah!

Elizabeth What's the matter?

Major (*clutching his face*) Nothing, just a twinge. I get them from time to time. You'd better get down to the shops quickly.

Elizabeth Why quickly?

Major Before they run out of food. They're always short on Mondays.

Elizabeth That's true.

Major Off you go then. (*He ushers her to the front door and opens it*) You don't want to miss what there is.

Elizabeth Oh, my handbag. (*She starts to turn back*)

Major I'll get it.

Elizabeth I'm perfectly capable of getting my own handbag, thank you. (*She goes to the bed and picks up her handbag*)

The Major runs behind her to the négligé, whips it off the door and stuffs it up his cardigan

What are you doing?

Major Nothing.

Elizabeth What's that you're hiding?

Major Er . . . something you mustn't see.

Elizabeth Why mustn't I see it?

Major Because you mustn't know about it. It's secret.

Elizabeth Secret? You mean it's a surprise?

Major Yes, it would be a surprise for you.

Elizabeth A surprise for me? Oh good, you know I love surprises. Show me.

Major I can't. I mustn't. You might be cross.

Elizabeth Why should I be cross? I'm never cross when people buy me presents.

Major Well it was very expensive.

Elizabeth But you know I love expensive things. Let me see it. I can't wait to get my hands on it.

Major Well you can have a quick look if you like. (*He pulls out the négligé and holds it up*)

Elizabeth Oh it's lovely. (*She takes it*) How sweet of you. I shall go and try it on at once.

Major You can't take it away.

Elizabeth Why not? You've just given it to me.

Major But I shouldn't have done, because . . . because it's for your birthday.

Elizabeth My birthday isn't for another six months.

Major Exactly. That's why I can't give it to you now.

Elizabeth Well you just *have*, and it's very nice of you. I'm very touched. I didn't think you'd still buy me presents now we're divorced.

Major I didn't mean to.

Elizabeth But you couldn't help yourself. You're such a kind man, Alan, spending all this money on me. If I'd have known I wouldn't have pestered you for the rent. This must have cost a fortune.

Major Oh my God! And I'll have to replace it.

Elizabeth What do you mean replace it?

Major Replace the money I've spent on that. It was the rent money.

Elizabeth Oh don't worry about that, pay me when you can. Oh, I am a fool! I've just realized. The night-dress in Teddy.

Major What about it?

Elizabeth It's a matching set. How clever of you. And you hid it in Teddy so I wouldn't find it. (*She picks up the night-dress from the bed*)

Major You're not taking that as well are you?

Elizabeth It's half the set, no point in having one without the other. I haven't had such a lovely surprise for a long time.

Major It's been a surprise for me as well. I think I've had enough surprises for one day.

Philip comes down the area steps carrying a holdall, which contains his barrister's gown etc. He is dressed as before, and is now very angry

The Major sees him, shuts the front door and bolts it. Philip puts his key in the door and finds he cannot open it

Elizabeth What did you do that for? Who's that?

Major It's the plumber.

Philip starts to bang on the door

Philip (*outside the door*) Open this door, Major.

Elizabeth He sounds pretty mad to me.

Major Pretty mad. There's nothing pretty about his madness—he's ugly mad. That's why I bolted the door.

Elizabeth You'll have to let him in.

Major Not while you're here.

Elizabeth Why ever not?

Philip (*outside*) Let me in. I demand you let me enter.

Elizabeth I think he's getting madder.

Major He is every second. It's you. You're a woman and he's woman-mad.

Elizabeth I'll ring the police.

Major No you mustn't. He'll quieten down if you go away.

Philip (*outside*) I'll break the door down.

Major I'm coming!

Elizabeth Ridiculous. Employing a man like that. Something should be done about him. He should be up in court.

Major He is, all the time. But he's a first-class plumber. Really knows his stuff.

Elizabeth That's something I suppose. I hope he won't be here for long.

Major I'll get rid of him as quickly as I can. You go upstairs. Try your nightie on.

Elizabeth I'm certainly not staying down here with him. You must be out of your mind letting him in here in the first place.

Major Yes I was. I only did it for money.

Elizabeth What?

Major I only did it for the money he charges, he's amazingly cheap. Off you go. (*He opens the door* UL *and ushers her off*)

Elizabeth exits

He closes the door, crosses to the front door and opens it. Philip bursts in

Philip Scared aren't you. I'm not surprised you bolted the door. I've a good mind to punch your head in.

Major What for? I haven't done anything.

Philip I had to apologize to Brenda's father for making her pregnant.

Major So you should. It wasn't a very nice thing to do.

Philip But I didn't.

Major Then why did you apologize?

Philip Because you told me he already knew. You said you'd spoken to him on the phone.

Major (*ruefully*) I . . . yes, I remember I did, didn't I.

Philip But you never did, did you?

Major Didn't I? Must have been a wrong number.

Philip Fine time to tell me that. The damage is done now.

Major I should say it is. You made Brenda pregnant.

Philip I didn't.

Major You said you did.

Philip No *you* said I did.

Major How would I know if you did or you didn't.

Philip You couldn't. That's why you shouldn't have interfered. I admitted liability to Brenda's father for something of which I was not culpable. And you can't expect justice from a man like Humphrey Bennett QC.

Major You mean you were entirely innocent?

Philip Not entirely, but neither was she. It was a case of *mutuus consensus*.

Major That was no use, you still got her pregnant.

Philip I keep telling you, I didn't.

Major Why didn't you tell her father?

Philip I did, but he wouldn't listen to me. He was furious. He took my briefs away from me, threw me out of chambers, and told me I must never see Brenda again.

Major Poor Brenda. She'll be an unmarried mother.

Philip How many times do I have to tell you. She is not pregnant. At least I don't think she is.

Major But you're not sure.

Philip I can't be, can I? I haven't spoken to Brenda yet. And now I shan't have a chance to. It was all your fault.

Major Good heavens, *I'm* not the father. I've never even met the girl.

Philip No, and you never will, I'll make sure of that. I'm getting out of here.

Major You're leaving?

Philip Yes. Thanks to you I shall have to go back to the Midlands and pick up what I can in the Magistrates' Court.

Major How soon are you going?

Philip You can't wait to see the back of me, can you?

Major No. I mean, no that's not true. Shall I help you pack?

Philip I'm not leaving until the morning. Now if you'll excuse me, I might as well put something more casual on. (*He goes towards the cupboard*)

Major (*panicking*) I shouldn't do that. I mean, you look very smart as you are. (*He gets between Philip and the cupboard*)

Philip I can't lounge about the flat in these clothes.

Major No you can't. Why don't you go for a walk in them instead.

Philip What do I want to go walking for?

Major It'll take your mind off Brenda.

Philip My mind *is* off Brenda. *Right* off her. I don't care what you say, I'm going to change. (*He goes determinedly to the cupboard door. He is about to open it*)

Major No, don't look in there!

Philip Why not?

Major Because they're not your clothes in there.

Philip What are you saying? Are you suggesting I stole them?

Major No, but your clothes aren't in there. I know they're not.

Philip You mean someone's stolen *my* clothes?

Major No, but they're not there.

Philip Where are they then? What have you done with them?

Major I . . . er . . . I took them to the cleaners.

Philip What did you do that for? They've just *been* cleaned.

Major I didn't know that, did I? They looked pretty dirty to me.

Philip Why have you been examining my clothes?

Major I had to. After the plumber. He made a terrible mess over every-thing. So I took your clothes to the cleaners.

Philip I can't see any mess.

Major No it's been cleaned up . . . by my cleaning lady. Did I tell you about my cleaning lady?

Philip You mean the unfrocked nun?

Major That's the one. So you go into the bathroom and take your clothes off, and I'll get your clothes from outside . . . I mean from outside the cleaners.

Philip Why on earth should I go into the bathroom and take my clothes off?

Major So that I can take *them* to the cleaners too.

Philip There's nothing wrong with these, they don't need cleaning

Major They've got a special offer on. Four suits for the price of three. And I've only taken them three, so there's another one to go.

Philip Oh, very well. I'll put my dressing-gown on.

Major You can't, that's at the cleaners too.

Philip Then I'll sit here in my underwear.

Major No! My cleaning lady's coming back. You remember she's terrified of men, particularly in their underwear.

Philip I thought you said she was a nun?

Major She was, but the monastery was next door, and they had a very low wall.

Philip Oh very well. I might as well have that shower I missed this morning.

He goes into the bathroom and shuts the door

The Major goes towards the cupboard. The phone rings. He quickly goes to it and picks up the receiver

Major Hallo? . . . Brenda! . . . No he isn't here. He's in the bath— gone to Bath. . . . But it's true. . . . No, don't come here, Brenda. . . . You mustn't meet. . . . Brenda, don't do that!

Philip opens the bathroom door and pokes his head out

Philip Did you say Brenda?

The Major slams down the receiver

Major No, it's the butcher. I said, "I must have meat, tender not too fat!"

Philip Oh!

He closes the bathroom door as he retreats inside

The Major crosses to the cupboard then remembers something. He goes over to the phone, takes the receiver off the hook and then returns to the cupboard

Philip opens the bathroom door and holds out his pinstripe trousers and black jacket

Major, my clothes.

Major I'm just doing them. Oh, I see what you mean. (*He takes the clothes*)

Philip goes back into the bathroom, closing the door again

The Major puts the jacket and trousers into the cupboard. He emerges from the cupboard bringing out an armful of Jill's clothes

As he does so, Humphrey Bennett QC comes down the area steps. Humphrey is a burly, overbearing man in his mid-fifties. He is dressed in black jacket and pinstripes, bowler hat, etc. He knocks on the door

The Major freezes, then, reluctant to answer the knock, he creeps up towards the door UL. Humphrey peers through the window and sees him

Humphrey Hallo in there. Can't you hear I'm knocking?

The Major reluctantly goes over to the door and opens it

(*As he enters*) Elizabeth?

Major No, Alan.

Humphrey Not you, you fool. Mrs Chelmsford-Smythe.

Major Oh you mean Elizabeth.

Humphrey That's right. Bit old for a Captain, aren't you?

Major I'm not a Captain, I'm a Major.

Humphrey Don't look any too young for that either. Humphrey Bennett QC, I've come about the flat.

Major Humphrey Bennett? You must be Philip Clarke's CO.

Humphrey Don't mention that name to me. He's brought shame on my family. Abused my trust. I threw him out of chambers.

Major Yes I know. He made your daughter pregnant, didn't he.

Humphrey You know about that? The whole of London must know. How did you find out?

Major Philip told me.

Humphrey The little swine. Not content with ruining my daughter, now he wants to ruin her name as well. I'd like to get my hands on him. Do you know where I can find him?

Major Yes, he's in the . . . he's in the Midlands.

Humphrey Gone to ground, has he? Just as well for him. Right, where's the flat I'm supposed to see?

Major This is it. Elizabeth didn't tell me about you.

Humphrey She phoned me only a quarter of an hour ago. Asked her if she knew of any accommodation. I'm an old friend of her father's, the General you know.

Major No, I didn't know.

Humphrey Aren't you going to show me round?

Major Yes of course. (*He puts the clothes on the bed*)

Humphrey Elizabeth told me the flat was empty.

Major It is.

Humphrey Then whose are those clothes?

Major They belong to a lady.

Humphrey I can see that. They're ladies' clothes.

Major I'm just moving them out for you. You won't tell Elizabeth, will you?

Humphrey What? Oh I get your point. No. You can rely on me. Soul of tact. We're both men of the world.

Major It's not like that.

Humphrey Of course not. That's what we all say when they smell a rat, don't we. Elizabeth on to your little game, is she?

Major No, no, she doesn't know a thing about it.

Humphrey Don't worry, she won't hear anything from me. (*He crosses to the bathroom door*) What's in here, the kitchen?

Major No, it's the bathroom.

Humphrey (*trying the door*) It's locked. Must be somebody in there.

Major Oh, so there is.

Humphrey You don't have to pretend with me. Likes bathroom games, does she? Rather partial to them myself.

Major She?

Humphrey Haven't got a man in there, have you? That's going too far. I'd have to tell Elizabeth about that.

Major No, no it's not a man.

Humphrey I didn't think it would be, did I. Must apologize for interrupting your bit of fun. Mustn't keep a man from his sport. I've seen enough. I'll take the flat.

Major You can't do that. There's someone here already.

Humphrey I don't mean right away. I'll move in tomorrow.

Major You can't do that, it's already let.

Humphrey Nonsense. When I spoke to Elizabeth just now on the telephone, she said I could definitely have it. I'd better have a word with her.

Major You can't. She's not here. She's gone out.

Humphrey I'll wait till she comes back.

Major She's not coming back. She's gone out . . . to Saudi Arabia.

Humphrey She said she wasn't going till tomorrow.

Major Yes, but tomorrow's flight was cancelled, so she took one today instead.

Humphrey (*surprised*) Aren't you going with her?

Major No, she doesn't want me.

Humphrey Oh, chucked you over, has she?

Major Yes, I'm afraid she did.

Humphrey So I can't have the flat then?

Major No, I'm afraid not.

Humphrey Pity. It would have suited me down to the ground. Not that three hundred pounds a month's cheap, when you consider I only want it for the odd night or two during the week.

Major During the week? You mean *not* at *weekends*?

Humphrey Well of course not. I have to put up with the wife from Friday night till Monday morning. That's more than enough for any man.

Major Yes, but I suppose a chap has to do his duty at weekends?

Humphrey Absolutely. *Familias super omnes.* Don't you agree?

Major I don't know really. What does it mean?

Humphrey Family above all, old chap. But only at weekends.

Major If that's the case, I think I might be able to accommodate you.

Humphrey I don't follow you?

Major The person who was going to take the flat hasn't left a deposit. So I suppose legally it hasn't been secured.

Humphrey Yes. Quite right. *Nihil securitas est.* Take my point?

Major Er . . . no.

Humphrey Why not?

Major I don't know what it means.

Humphrey (*taking out his wallet*) It means that I'm going to give you a month's rent in advance, which means the flat's mine. (*He gives the Major the money*) Three hundred pounds.

Major Oh, thank you very much.

Humphrey You can let me have a receipt in the morning. I'll drop my stuff in about ten, on my way to chambers.

Major I'll have everything cleared out by then.

Humphrey Good. I hope I can rely on your discretion, old chap, about all this. One has to be very careful in my position.

Major Yes, I've got to be pretty careful in mine.

Humphrey Quite understand, old chap. We're both tarred with the same brush, eh? Both paddling the same canoe?

Major How do you mean?

Humphrey (*indicating the bathroom*) You know, water sports. I won't keep you. I'm sure you don't want the water to get cold. (*Indicating the kitchen*) Is this the kitchen?
Major Yes.
Humphrey Mind if I have a peep before I go?
Major By all means.

Humphrey goes into the kitchen, leaving the door open, as ...

Philip comes out of the bathroom with a towel round him

Philip (*impatiently*) Haven't you brought my clothes back yet?
Major Just going to get them.
Elizabeth (*off* UL) Alan, are you still down there?
Major Quick, it's my cleaning lady. Get in there. (*He pushes Philip back into the bathroom*)

Philip exits

The Major shuts the door

As he does so, Humphrey comes out of the kitchen

Humphrey I think this place will suit me splendidly. I shall only be using it on an *ad hoc* basis.

The Major goes to the front door and holds it open

Major You've seen it now and I'll see you tomorrow ... (*He suddenly sees ...*)

Jill coming down the area steps

(*Hastily shutting the door*) Oh my God. You haven't seen the fire escape, useful in emergencies.

He dashes downstage and bundles Humphrey into the kitchen, following him in, and shutting the door behind him

At this moment, Jill opens the front door and enters, carrying her suitcase and handbag. She puts it on the bed and sees her clothes

Jill What on earth ... ?

She picks up the clothes and goes into the cupboard with them

The door UL *opens and Elizabeth comes in wearing the night-dress and négligé*

Elizabeth What do you think, Alan? Oh, he's gone.

She goes out of the UL *door, leaving it open*

The Major comes out of the kitchen, shutting the door behind him

Major Jill, I'm sorry ...

He sees the door UL *open, and dashes out of it*

Jill comes out of the cupboard, carrying one or two clothes which she hasn't yet hung up

Jill Alan?

She sees that no-one is there, and goes back into the cupboard

The Major runs in from UL *carrying Philip's black jacket and pinstripes. He opens the bathroom door and throws them inside*

Major Here's your clothes. (*He shuts the door as . . .*)

Jill comes out of the cupboard again

Jill Oh, there you are.
Major You can't stay here.

Elizabeth comes in through the door UL

Elizabeth What do you think, Alan? (*She does a twirl*)
Jill My night-dress!

Philip comes out of the bathroom, holding his black jacket and pinstripes

Philip I don't want these. (*He sees Elizabeth*) Oh my God!
Elizabeth The mad plumber!
Philip The naughty nun!

He runs back into the bathroom and Elizabeth runs off UL *as . . .*

Humphrey comes out of the kitchen. He hears the bathroom door slam and then sees Jill

Humphrey (*to the Major*) Good God. Two at a time! Talk about the galloping Major!

The CURTAIN *falls*

ACT II

SCENE 1

The same. The action is continuous

Humphrey You've certainly got plenty on your plate, old boy.

Major No, no, it isn't like that at all.

Jill She had my night-dress and négligé on.

Humphrey You mean the bird in the bathroom?

Jill No, the one from upstairs.

Humphrey My God, three! How do you do it?

Major It does get a bit confusing.

Jill I want to know what's going on.

Humphrey More like what's coming off, eh? (*He chuckles knowingly*)

Jill I beg your pardon?

Humphrey (*confidentially to the Major*) And you only married a few months. How d'you get away with it?

Major (*surprised*) I'm not married.

Humphrey (*looking at Jill; aside to the Major*) Oh quite. See what you mean. Best thing, don't let on you're married, can't blackmail you then.

Jill When you two have quite finished muttering, perhaps you'll be kind enough to give me an explanation. Major, who is this man?

Humphrey Don't worry about me, my dear. I'm nothing to do with your little foursome, but I hope the Major will count me in sometime. (*To the Major*) Now I know why the army keeps you fighting fit. Talk about join the professionals!

He goes out of the front door, and off up the area steps

Jill What the hell's going on in my flat? Major. I come back here to find a naked man in my bathroom, a dirty old man in my living-room and a cheap woman in my night-dress.

Major There's nothing cheap about Elizabeth.

Jill Oh. She's your kept woman is she?

Major She's not a kept woman. She's my ex-wife. Mind you, there's not much difference.

Jill Why have you given your ex-wife my clothes?

Major They're not yours. They may look like yours, but I assure you they're not yours.

Jill Then where are mine?

Major I . . . er . . . took them to the cleaners.

Jill What?! They're supposed to be handwashed in lukewarm water. They'll be ruined. They were brand new.

Major Yes, that's why I was so upset when the plumber made all that mess and got them dirty. You remember I told you about the plumber?

Jill Yes. Where is he? I want a word with him.

Major You can't, he's gone.

Jill Well somebody's got to pay for it. That night-set cost me two hundred and fifty pounds.

Major Did it? No wonder she was pleased. Look, I'll get your set back from her . . . her, the lady at the cleaners . . . and if there's anything wrong with it, I promise I'll give you two hundred and fifty pounds. I've got it here. (*He brings out the money he got from Humphrey, and shows it to her*)

Jill Well I suppose that's better than nothing. And while we're about it why were all my clothes on the bed?

Major I was checking them, to see if they needed to go to the cleaners too. But luckily they didn't.

Jill The man in my bathroom. Where's he come from?

Major Er . . . he's come from . . . upstairs.

Jill Upstairs?

Major Yes. You see when the plumber fixed the plumbing down here, he accidentally upset the plumbing up there. It's very old plumbing and very easily upset. So I told that man in the bathroom he could bath down here.

Jill He lives upstairs?

Major Er . . . yes.

Jill He must be living with your ex-wife.

Major Yes he must.

Jill Then he must be her new husband.

Major Must he? Yes, he must.

Jill Then he's the adjutant— your best friend.

Major Is he? Oh, God yes, he must be.

Jill I'm surprised you let them in your house, after what they've done to you.

Major That's just it. You see it's not my house. It belongs to my ex-wife.

Jill But you said it was yours when you rented me the flat.

Major I had to. I know I shouldn't have done, but I needed the money. I couldn't get a job when I left the army. I was broke and Elizabeth made me pay for the upkeep of the whole house. And I had to pay rent on top. I didn't know what to do.

Jill She sounds a very hard women.

Major Oh, no, she's not all that bad.

Jill You're much too charitable, Alan, that's your trouble. You just leave her and her husband to me. I'll sort them out.

Major No please don't. There's no need. There's no time. They're going to Saudi Arabia tomorrow.

Jill You'll be well rid of them.

Major I'd like to part on good terms. So if you wouldn't mind not saying anything to my wife, about me letting you have the flat . . . ?

Jill If that's the way you want it.

Major I would prefer it. If you could stay in a hotel just for tonight, they need never know what I've been up to. I'll pay of course. I wouldn't ask you do do it if it wasn't absolutely essential.

Jill I think you ought to stand up to them.

Major You don't know them. They're a devious couple. They might sell the house. Then where would I be?

Jill I wouldn't like to see you thrown out on the street. I mean you've done nothing to deserve it, Alan.

Major Then you don't mind going?

Jill No, not if it's only for one night. As long as I can come back here tomorrow.

Major You can and you can't.

Jill What do you mean?

Major You *can* come back, but you *can't* come back here, not to this flat.

Jill What! Why not?

Major Because Elizabeth has let the flat. But it's all right, because when they've gone, you can have the whole of upstairs, apart from my room.

Jill They? You mean your ex-wife and that creep of a husband of hers in the bathroom.

Major Er . . . yes. It's very nice upstairs.

Jill How much is that going to cost me, for goodness sake?

Major Nothing at all. I've treated you very badly. I couldn't take money from you now. You're much too nice.

Jill I couldn't.

Major You must. I insist. I want you to.

Jill How can I say no? I'm glad I came back from Highgate, in more ways than one.

Major How was Highgate?

Jill Awful. Drink, drugs and debauchery.

Major Isn't that what you wanted?

Jill What sort of girl do you take me for?

Major (*embarrassed*) I didn't mean . . . I hope you didn't think I meant . . .

Jill I wouldn't blame you if you did. I should never have gone there. Divorce makes you do things you wouldn't have dreamt of.

Major Very true. I've done a few myself.

Jill Doesn't work out really, does it?

Major I don't know. It's beginning to.

Philip comes out of the bathroom, dressed in his black jacket and pinstripes

No it's not!

Philip What the blazes is going on? And who's she and what's she doing in here.

Major She's . . . she's . . .

Jill I'm his niece.

Major She's my niece. (*Realizing*) What!

Jill Uncle, we'd better be on our way to the hotel.

Major What hotel?

Jill The one I'm staying in tonight.

Major Oh that hotel. (*He picks up her suitcase from the bed*)

Philip Just a minute. I want a word with you.

Major Not in front of my niece.

Philip I don't give a damn about your niece. I'm only concerned with you—you've behaved disgracefully.

Jill You're a fine one to talk after what you and that female have been up to.

Philip He's told you, has he? Let me tell you, there's not a word of truth in it. He invented the whole thing.

Jill On the contrary, he defended you, which I think was very noble of him in the circumstances. I think the sooner you go to Saudi Arabia the better.

Philip What on earth do I want to go to Saudi Arabia for?

Major Parts of it are very nice, if you can get out of the sun.

Jill So it's all your wife's idea?

Major Well——

Philip My wife? I'm not even married.

Jill You're worse than I thought, you didn't even have the decency to marry her.

Major No he——

Philip I've no intention of marrying her now. Even if I wanted to her father wouldn't let me.

The phone rings. All three go towards the phone. The Major gets there first.

Major I'll get it. (*He picks up the receiver*) Hallo. .... Hallo, Brenda. (*To Philip*) It's Brenda.

Philip (*grabbing the phone*) Hallo, Brenda, it's me. I must know, are you pregnant? .... Don't be like that Brenda. I only asked. You're where? ... Waterloo? Shall I meet you there? ... Oh, all right then, I'll see you when you get here. (*He puts the receiver down*)

Major She's coming here?

Philip Yes, we're going to sort this business out once and for all. Brenda's hopping mad.

Jill I'm not surprised.

Philip I don't think she'll ever forgive me for this.

Major Oh yes she will. Go and buy her a nice bunch of flowers.

Jill Huh! The male answer to everything.

Philip Perhaps it isn't such a good idea after all.

Major Course it is. Brenda'll soon come round with a few dozen roses.

Philip It's worth a try I suppose.

Major Yes, you go off at once, before they sell out. There's a very good florist just round the corner, in Bond Street.

Philip That's miles away.

Major Not when you know the way. Off you go.

Philip goes out and up the area steps

Jill What a nasty piece of work. Not satisfied with running off with your ex-wife, now he's got this Brenda girl pregnant too.

Major Yes it would seem like that. Come on we'd better find you a hotel before Elizabeth comes down.

Jill But what about all my things?

Major Don't worry. I've got a way of dealing with those. You get your clothes out of the cupboard.

Jill Right.

She goes into the cupboard

The Major goes off UL, *brings on the three drawers containing Philip's clothes and swaps them for the three in the chest*

Jill comes out of the cupboard with an armful of her clothes

What are you doing?

Major Putting his clothes in here.

Jill His?

Major Er . . . the new tenant's. Take those out there. There's a cupboard out there you can hang them in. You'll find his stuff in there.

Jill goes off UL *carrying her clothes*

The Major completes the changeover of the drawers

Jill returns with Philip's clothes, which she hangs in the cupboard

The Major goes off UL *with the drawers*

Whilst this is going on, they speak the following

Jill You seem to have it well organized.

Major You have to if you're letting.

Jill Your new tenant must be a barrister.

Major Yes he is. How did you know?

Jill (*holding up a wig*) This wig.

Major Oh yes of course, he's one too.

Jill What do you mean, he's one too?

Major Er . . . he's won two cases this week. He's brilliant, never loses.

He picks up the drawers containing Jill's clothes and goes off UL

Jill I think you'd better introduce him to Brenda. She might need to take the adjutant to court.

She goes into the cupboard

The Major returns

Major What would she want to do that for?

Jill (*coming out*) For getting her pregnant.

Major Oh, that. I don't think it'll come to that. I've got a feeling it might turn out to be a phantom pregnancy. Right. All set? (*He picks up her suitcase*)

Jill Yes. (*She picks up her handbag*)

Major Come on then.

They make for the front door, as ...

  Elizabeth, now properly dressed, enters UL

Elizabeth Alan, where are you going?
Major Ah Elizabeth! Just taking Jill to her hotel.
Elizabeth And who might she be?
Major She's ... my niece, aren't you?
Jill Yes Uncle, I'm your niece.
Major My sister's daughter.
Elizabeth You're an only child.
Major Quite right.
Elizabeth Then how can she be your sister's daughter?
Major I didn't say "sister". I said "solicitor". (*He slurs it to sound like sister*)
  She's my solicitor's daughter.
Elizabeth (*to Jill*) Then you must be old Hargreaves' daughter.
Major That's right. She's old Hargreaves' young daughter. She isn't really
  my niece, but we're so close I think of her as my niece.
Elizabeth How nice. I remember you when you were only so high. You've
  changed a lot.
Jill Yes, I've grown up.
Elizabeth You used to have flaming red hair.
Jill I put it out. I mean I grew it out. It was dyed. This is my natural colour.
Elizabeth You must miss your father.
Jill Oh I do. It was a very sad bereavement.
Elizabeth Bereavement? He was sent to jail.
Major Of course he was, but they don't like to talk about it. It was such a
  terrible disgrace.
Elizabeth I never did find out exactly what they got him for? What did he
  do?
Major He was a solicitor.
Elizabeth No, what crime did he commit?
Jill Er ...
Major He cooked the books.
Jill Yes, then threw them in the fire.
Elizabeth What?
Major He tried to destroy the evidence. That made it worse for him.
Elizabeth How long did he get?
Jill } (*together*) { Five years.
Major } (*together*) { Three years.
Elizabeth Which? Five years or three years?
Major Both. To run concurrently.
Elizabeth How sad. Where is he?
Jill } (*together*) { Dartmoor.
Major } (*together*) { Wormwood Scrubs.
Major Er ... he was in Wormwood Scrubs, but they transferred him to
  Dartmoor, because ... because ...
Jill Because he didn't like it there.
Elizabeth Didn't like it there?

Major No, he didn't like it there, that's why he tried to escape. So they sent him to Dartmoor.

Elizabeth Do give him my regards when you next visit him in Dartmoor.

Jill Yes I will.

Elizabeth Alan, is that madman still in the bathroom?

Major No, he's gone.

Elizabeth Thank goodness for that. I hope he doesn't come back.

Major So do I.

Jill I'm not surprised the way he's treated you both. Are you still going to Saudi Arabia with him?

Elizabeth The plumber?

Major She's not going to Saudi Arabia with the plumber.

Jill No, I meant the adjutant.

Elizabeth Of course I am. After all he is my husband.

Jill Your husband? He told me you weren't married . . .

Major No, I don't think——

Elizabeth Not married? Why the devil should he say that?

Jill I think I know. (*To the Major*) Should we tell her?

Major (*baffled*) Tell her what?

Jill About Brenda.

Elizabeth Brenda? Who's Brenda?

Major Nobody you know.

Jill But I think you ought to know. She's on her way here now in a taxi, and he got her pregnant.

Elizabeth He got her pregnant in a taxi?!

Major (*desperate*) No that's not where it happened. It's all a mistake.

Elizabeth A mistake? I should think it is. He's at it again! He promised me he'd give it up when I married him.

Jill He obviously hasn't. Have you had a lot of trouble with him?

Elizabeth Yes I have. I should have known what kind of man he was, running off with another man's wife.

Jill Who was that?

Elizabeth Me!

Major At least he's done one decent thing in his life.

Elizabeth What's that supposed to mean?

Major I mean he did the decent thing by you, when he married you.

Elizabeth Oh yes? You mean now he's going to do the decent thing by this Brenda creature and marry *her*!

Major No, I don't think he'll do that. In fact I can almost guarantee it.

Elizabeth What do you know about it?

Major Nothing. But I do know Ronald. He's a very nice chap. Has his little weaknesses of course.

Elizabeth Yes, like about half a dozen a month. Well, Brenda's one too many. I'll teach him. I won't go to Saudi Arabia with him, I'll stay here.

Major What? You must go. Your promised him you would. I'll talk to him. I'm *certain* it's all a mistake. Don't you think so, Jill?

Jill Er . . . yes I do. You must go. Let Uncle sort it out with him.

Major Uncle who?

Jill You.

Major Yes of course. I'll sort it out with him. He'll listen to me.

Elizabeth Nobody ever listens to you Alan, you're far too nice. You're not like Ronald. You don't know how to tell a lie. I'd know straight away if you weren't telling me the truth.

Jill Uncle always tells the truth, don't you, Uncle?

Major Maybe not all the time.

Elizabeth Well, that's a lie for a start. You're transparently honest.

Major I think I might be getting a little bit opaque in my old age.

Elizabeth (*to Jill*) Tell me, my dear, did I hear "Uncle Alan" say he was taking you to a hotel?

Jill He is, yes.

Elizabeth What a pity we're so short of beds upstairs, otherwise I'd have been delighted for you to stay.

Jill How very kind of you.

Elizabeth Anyway, you must come upstairs for a drink before you go, then we can have a nice long chat about old times.

Major She doesn't want to talk about old times. She doesn't even understand them.

Jill I don't mind at all. In fact I'd enjoy it.

Major I don't think I would. I expect you've forgotten most of it.

Elizabeth Just because you've got a bad memory, it doesn't mean to say everybody else has.

Major I seem to have more things to remember than most people, especially recently.

Elizabeth Have you remembered to move your clothes?

Major Have I? (*He looks quickly in the drawer*) No I haven't. But I hadn't forgotten.

Elizabeth Well get on and do it. (*She goes towards the door* UL. *To Jill*) There are so many questions I'm dying to ask you.

Major (*panic-stricken*) I'll come with you.

Elizabeth What on earth for?

Major In case she can't remember the answers.

Jill Don't worry, Uncle. I'm sure I can manage.

Elizabeth Come along. I'll bring your case.

Jill Thank you.

Elizabeth We can go up this way. (*She opens the* UL *door*)

Jill passes her and goes off

Major I'll carry that. (*He picks up Jill's suitcase*)

Elizabeth No, no. You've got to move your clothes out of here, remember?

She takes Jill's case from the Major and goes out UL

Major But I . . . don't you . . . (*Resignedly he takes off his jacket and hangs it behind the door* UL. *He goes to the cupboard and starts to take out Philip's clothes*)

Philip is seen coming down the area steps

The Major takes a large bundle of clothes out UL

As he disappears Philip enters through the front door, carrying a large bouquet of flowers

The Major returns immediately

He doesn't see Philip and goes to the chest of drawers and starts to scoop up Philip's clothes. He is half-way through this operation when he catches sight of Philip. He quickly puts the clothes back and starts to smooth them out

Moths. I thought I heard moths in your drawers, and if you get moths in your drawers you get holes in your drawers . . . (*He peters out*)
Philip Moths don't eat nylon.
Major Exactly. They were making a lot of noise because they were frustrated, and I heard them.
Philip Sounds very far-fetched to me. Have you got my clothes back from the cleaners? (*He puts the flowers down on the bed*)
Major Yes.

Philip goes to the cupboard and opens it, to find it empty

Philip It's empty.
Major Yes, it is. I had to take them back. They'd done a very shoddy job.
Philip I want them back at once. I never asked you to take them in the first place. It's a damn cheek.
Major Just a minute. I'll go and get them back. They should be ready now. They're express cleaners.

He goes out UL *and returns immediately with clothes*

How about that for express service. I knew you'd want them back so I'd already collected them. (*He puts the clothes on the bed*)
Philip I'm not going to pay.
Major I wouldn't expect you to. I mean it wasn't your fault the plumber made such a mess.
Philip At least you seem to have cleaned up the place satisfactorily.
Major It was a pleasure . . . No! We haven't started yet. My cleaning lady is on her way now.
Philip Can't she wait until I've changed. (*He starts to sort out some clothes to wear*)
Major No she won't wait. She's like a whirlwind. Nothing stops her when she gets going.
Philip Can't she clean round me?
Major Certainly not. I've told you before she's terrified of men.
Philip I suppose I'll have to go into the bathroom again.
Major Yes. That would be best. We don't want to upset her, do we?
Philip I suppose not. Where are my shoes? (*He has collected his clothes by now*)
Major (*indicating* UL) Out there.
Philip What are they doing out there?

Major Well you see. I took them to the cobblers to have them cobbled, but he said they didn't need cobbling, so I brought them back. I'll get them.

He goes out UL

Philip Why can't you leave my things alone?

The Major returns with two pairs of shoes

Major I promise I won't touch them again.
Philip Thank you.

He takes one pair of shoes from the Major and goes into the bathroom, shutting the door behind him

The Major immediately hurls the other pair of shoes off UL, *grabs the clothes and the bouquet off the bed and runs off* UL *with them, as . . .*

Brenda comes down the area steps. She knocks on the front door

The Major returns, goes to the chest and opens the drawer

Brenda knocks again, louder. The Major dithers, then goes to open the front door. Brenda walks in. Brenda Bennett is a pretty, well-groomed and well-dressed girl in her mid-twenties

Brenda Is Mr Philip Clarke here?
Major Who wants him?
Brenda I'm Brenda Bennett.
Major Ah yes, he's expecting you. He's gone round to the pub. He said could you meet him there.
Brenda Which pub?
Major Er . . . I'm not sure, he didn't say. But if you try them all round here, you're bound to find him.
Brenda I'm certainly not going on a pub crawl looking for him. I shall wait here till he comes back.
Major You can't do that. I've got the cleaning woman coming in.
Brenda Are you his landlord, the Major, the man I spoke to on the phone?
Major Er . . . what did I say?
Brenda You told me not to come here. Why did you tell me that?
Major I didn't tell you that. That wasn't me. I'm not the Major.
Brenda You're not? Surely that's a military tie you're wearing?
Major Yes it is, because I was in the army, but I'm not a major.
Brenda Who are you then and what are you doing in Philip's flat?
Major I'm from upstairs. I live there with the Major.
Brenda What's your name?
Major Er . . . Chelmsford-Smythe.

A taxi horn honks impatiently outside

Brenda Oh, I must pay off my taxi.
Major Yes I should.

She runs off and up the area steps

The Major shuts the front door behind her, dashes to the chest and starts to take out the clothes as ...

   Elizabeth, wearing a pretty overall and a headscarf and carrying a light-weight vacuum cleaner, enters UL

Elizabeth Haven't you cleared out your clothes, yet?

Major Just doing it. Why don't you come back in half an hour when I've done it?

Elizabeth Don't be ridiculous. Get on with it while I start on the bathroom.

Major No! There's someone in there.

Elizabeth Someone in there? Who?

Major The plumber.

Elizabeth Not again? I thought you got rid of him.

Major I did. He's come back. He wanted to check his work. But don't worry I'll tell him to go away, while you start on the kitchen.

   Brenda comes down the area steps

Elizabeth And this time, make sure he *stays* away. I'm not having a sex-mad plumber in my house. (*She goes towards the kitchen*)

There is a knock on the front door. The Major freezes

   Well, aren't you going to answer it?

Major No, I'm sure it's no-one important.

Elizabeth How do you know that?

Major I didn't recognize the knock.

There is another knock

   No, I still don't recognize it.

Elizabeth Have you gone mad, Alan? Answer the door.

Major I'd rather not.

Elizabeth Then I will. (*She goes to the front door*)

Major I'd rather you didn't.

   Elizabeth opens the front door and Brenda walks in, carrying a suitcase

Brenda Oh!

Elizabeth Can I help you?

Brenda No, I can manage. Don't let me interrupt your cleaning.

Elizabeth I don't think we've met before, have we?

Brenda No.

Major This is Miss Bennett.

Elizabeth Miss Bennett?

Major You know, Humphrey Bennett's daughter.

Elizabeth Oh I see. How nice to meet you. I never knew Humphrey had a daughter. I expect you've come to have a peep at the flat.

Brenda Yes, in a way. (*To the Major*) Who is this lady?

Major She's Mrs Chelmsford-Smythe.

Brenda (*to Elizabeth*) Oh I do apologize. I thought you were the cleaning lady.

Elizabeth I quite understand, dressed like this. Is your father here with you?
Brenda No. I'm afraid we're not on speaking terms at the moment.
Elizabeth I'm sorry to hear that. But he will come round won't he?
Brenda Yes I'm sure he will in his own good time.
Elizabeth I hope he makes it today. I'm leaving in the morning.
Brenda I don't understand.
Major Mrs Chelmsford-Smythe's going to Saudi Arabia in the morning.
Elizabeth Yes, with my husband.
Brenda (*to the Major*) That'll be nice for you both.
Major Yes it'll be nice for all of us.
Elizabeth Alan, will you get that man out of the bathroom?
Major No, not yet.
Elizabeth Hadn't you better do something about it?
Major Yes, but just at the moment, he's best left where he is.
Brenda There's someone in the bathroom?
Major Er—we're having trouble with the plumbing. That's why we're down
here. Why don't we all go upstairs?
Elizabeth Yes, come up and have a drink.
Brenda Thank you all the same, but I'd rather wait here for Philip.
Elizabeth Philip?
Brenda My fiancé. Your husband told me he's gone round to the pub.
Elizabeth My husband? I didn't know you knew my husband.
Brenda I didn't. Until just now.
Elizabeth Alan, you didn't tell me Ronnie had come back.
Major There wasn't any point. He only popped in for a minute and then
popped out again.
Elizabeth But I wanted to talk to him.
Brenda I can't understand why Philip's gone to a pub. He doesn't even like
them.

*Philip comes out of the bathroom, fully dressed in casual clothes. He is
carrying the clothes he has taken off*

Philip Brenda!
Brenda Philip. I thought you were in the pub.
Major So did I. Just shows we can all make mistakes.
Elizabeth Excuse me, your name's Brenda?
Brenda Yes, that's right.
Major Not *that* Brenda.
Brenda What Brenda?
Major The one I told Elizabeth about. She was a different Brenda.
Elizabeth That's a relief.
Brenda Who's Elizabeth?
Elizabeth I am. Have you finished in the bathroom, young man?
Philip Yes. You can get on with your cleaning now.
Elizabeth You don't have to tell me what to do, thank you very much.
Philip No need to be frightened of me. I shan't interfere with you.
Elizabeth You'd better not. One false move and I'll send for the police.
Brenda Do you two know each other?

Major They do and they don't.
Brenda What do you mean?
Major They do know each other but they don't know each other very well.
Brenda Then you don't know that Philip's my fiancé?
Elizabeth Your fiancé? I'm terribly sorry for you.
Brenda (*puzzled*) Sorry?
Elizabeth After what he's done? You must know what sort of man he is.
Philip After what I've done?
Major You know what you've done. You told me all about it.
Philip I told you I hadn't done it. It was all a mistake.
Brenda Then why did you tell Daddy I was pregnant?
Philip I didn't tell your father anything of the sort. (*Pointing to the Major*) He did.
Elizabeth Why did you say that, Alan?
Major I didn't. (*Pointing to Philip*) He did.
Brenda Why did you do that? There was no need to tell him at all.
Elizabeth It's not the sort of secret you can keep for very long.
Major You might as well tell everybody, Brenda. They'll all know sooner or later.
Brenda I'm not. It's all a mistake.
Elizabeth It always is.
Philip It seems to me I'm the last to know. You might have told me.
Brenda Why should I lie to you?
Philip I don't know. That's why it's so hurtful.
Brenda I really don't know what you're talking about, Philip. But I think it's something we ought to discuss in private.
Major I think that would be safer ... er better.
Elizabeth Yes, I'm sure you two have got a lot to sort out. Harrods have got some lovely layettes. I tell you what, why don't you stay down here and talk things over. Come on, Alan, we'll leave them on their own.
Major Yes. I can't seen any reason why we shouldn't
Elizabeth If you need anything, just give us a shout.

She goes out UL

Major (*to Philip*) You won't be wanting to change again, will you?
Philip No. Should I?
Major No, you shouldn't. You look fine as you are.

He goes out UL *shutting the door behind him*

Brenda I think you've got a nerve telling everyone I'm pregnant when I'm not.
Philip You're not?
Brenda Of course I'm not. You don't think I'm stupid do you?
Philip Your father thinks you are.
Brenda What, stupid?
Philip No, pregnant.
Brenda Of course he does. You told him I was, didn't you.
Philip But I thought you were. That's what the Major said.

Brenda Your landlord? It's nothing to do with him. How would he know?

Philip He said your father phoned up and said there was trouble, and it was something to do with you.

Brenda So you thought it was *that* sort of trouble.

Philip What else was I to think?

Brenda Almost anything but *that* I would have thought.

Philip I wouldn't have thought that, naturally, but for the Major. He seemed so certain.

Brenda So it was all his doing?

Philip Yes. It's beginning to look like that.

Brenda I knew it. I knew it when I spoke to him on the phone there was something shifty about him. I don't know what it is, but he's up to something.

Philip Yes, he has been behaving very oddly today.

Brenda Then there was the other time I phoned and a girl answered. She said you were kinky and dressed up in women's clothes and were thrown out.

Philip What?! There's something very odd going on around here. Do you know, he keeps stealing my clothes.

Brenda Perhaps *he's* kinky.

Philip I don't know, but I'm going to keep a pretty sharp eye on him from now on. I wouldn't trust him further than I could punch him. At least I've got my clothes back now. (*He opens the cupboard door and looks in*) My God! They've gone again! I've had enough of this nonsense. (*He goes to the* UL *door and opens it*)

The Major, who has been listening outside the door, almost falls in

What the hell are you playing at?

Major I . . . er . . . you . . . er . . . I thought you'd like these.

He produces the bouquet. Philip takes it

Philip What have you done with my stuff! I thought I told you to leave it there. (*He points to the cupboard*)

Major Oh, I thought you told me to leave it bare. So I took them out. Don't worry I'll bring them back right away.

He goes out of the UL *door and returns immediately with the clothes, which he dumps in Philip's arms*

Here you are.

He quickly goes out UL *and shuts the door*

Brenda How nice of him to give you some flowers.

Philip He didn't. They're for you. (*He puts the clothes on the bed*)

Brenda Well it's nice of him to give them to you to give to me.

Philip But they're not his, they're mine. I got them to give to you.

Brenda Then why did you give them to him?

Philip I didn't. I give up. They're yours anyway. (*He gives them to her*)

Brenda What a lovely surprise, darling. They're beautiful. Now *I've* got a little surprise for *you*.

Philip You have?

Brenda (*picking up her suitcase*) This.

Philip (*taking it*) That's very nice of you, I wanted a new case.

Brenda No, silly, they're my things. I've come to stay with you.

Philip You're moving in?

Brenda If you'd like me to?

Philip Of course I would.

Brenda That's settled. But before I do, I want everything open and above board. We've had enough trouble with Daddy as it is. We'll go round and see him right away.

Philip Do you think that's wise? He threw me out.

Brenda He'll have to take you back. Come on, there's no time like the present. (*She takes his hand and leads him to the front door*) I'll pay for the taxi.

They go out and off up the area steps

There is a knock on the door UL. *After a moment, Elizabeth opens the door and steps in*

Elizabeth I wonder if . . . Hallo! Anyone at home? (*She sees the clothes on the bed, exasperated*) Oh!

She takes the clothes and Brenda's case off UL. *She returns, opens the drawers of the chest, takes out whatever is left and takes them out* UL. *She returns once more and goes to the phone. She picks up the receiver and dials a number. After a moment or two, she inserts a coin in the box*

Hallo Humphrey. . . . It's Elizabeth Chelmsford-Smythe, again. I've been expecting you about the flat. . . . You've seen it? . . . You gave my husband three hundred pounds? He never told me. . . . I don't know why he should tell you that, you can come in any time you like. . . . Yes, this evening would be fine. We can have a chat then. . . . You've got a bit of business to do? . . . Well I'm sure we'll find a moment. Look forward to seeing you this evening. 'Bye. (*She puts the receiver down. She then takes a Yale key with a label attached out of her overall pocket, tries it in the front door lock and, satisfied it is the right one, she puts it on top of the chest. She plugs the vacuum cleaner in and starts to clean the carpet*)

The Major comes hurrying in UL

Major (*loudly*) Where have they gone? Did you see them? What did they say?

Elizabeth switches the cleaner off

Elizabeth There's no need to shout, Alan. What did you say?

Major Where are they?

Elizabeth They're not here any more. I just came down to ask if I could use the phone and found they'd gone.

Major That's odd. He told me he was going to stay.

Elizabeth Why should they stay? They've obviously sorted out their problems and gone off together.

Major I must say that's a great relief.

Elizabeth Yes. I'm pleased for them too. I like to see young people happy. We were happy once, weren't we, Alan?

Major Oh, yes, quite.

Elizabeth It was all Ronnie's fault. If I'd known then what I know now, I would never have gone away with him, let alone married him. You just don't know what I've been through, Alan.

Major No I don't.

Elizabeth This Brenda, whoever she is, isn't the only one, by any means.

Major I wouldn't be too hard on him. I don't think he really got her pregnant.

Elizabeth Don't you believe it. That's your trouble, Alan. You always think the best of everybody. I know Ronnie only too well. If it isn't birds it's betting, and if it isn't betting it's booze.

Ronald enters UL *rather the worse for drink*

Ronald Hallo Alan, my dear fellow. How very nice to see you. Couldn't lend us fifty quid, could you? Got a dead cert for the dogs tonight.

Major (*to Elizabeth*) At least he hasn't got a bird with him.

Elizabeth Ronald! Who is Brenda?

Ronald No, no, don't know any Brendas.

Elizabeth Let me jog your sozzled memory. She's probably young, almost certainly attractive and definitely pregnant. Does that help you at all?

Ronald No. But I like the sound of the first two-thirds of her.

Elizabeth Can't keep your hands off them, can you. Was she another bit of canteeen crumpet.

Ronald I don't know what she's talking about, do you, old boy?

Major I've no idea who Brenda is, and I'm sure she's not pregnant.

Elizabeth How do you know if you don't know her?

Major I don't know. I've just got a hunch about it.

Elizabeth You keep your hunches to yourself. Ronald, we'll continue this discussion in private, upstairs. And while you're there you can move your things out of my room. You can sleep in the spare room tonight. (*She goes* UL)

Major But the only other bed upstairs is mine.

Ronald That's all right, I'll sleep down here.

Elizabeth No you won't. You can sleep upstairs, on the floor!

She goes out UL

Ronald She's a hard woman, Alan.

Major The floor's even harder. She took the carpet as well.

Ronald You couldn't ... er ... go into the kitchen for a minute could you?

Major Whatever for?

Ronald I know, make me a cup of coffee. I could do with it.

Major Oh, all right.

He goes into the kitchen

Ronald Upstairs be blowed. I'm staying down here. (*He makes sure he is unobserved and quickly goes to the phone. He takes out his pocket address book, finds the number he wants, lifts the receiver and dials*) Hallo ... I'm calling Lorraine's Escort Agency, I want a girl for a bit of company. ... Oh, you're the operator? ... The number's been changed? What again? ... Hold on, I'll get a pen. (*He looks round, sees Alan's jacket hanging on the back of the door, fishes into the inside pocket and finds a pen and the £300. He goes back to the phone with both*) Right, fire ahead. ... (*He writes the number down in his book, putting the money in his pocket in order to give himself a free hand*) Thank you. (*He disconnects the call, then dials the number. After a moment, he inserts a coin*) Lorraine's Escort Agency? ... Ronald Chelmsford-Smythe. I'm an account customer. ... I'd like one of your lady companions to pop round about half-past ten this evening. ... Twelve-A Mortimer Crescent, Lancaster Gate. Make sure she comes to the garden flat. ... Thank you.

He puts down the receiver, and then goes to the bed and tests it with his hand for springiness. Satisfied, he goes towards the door UL, *thinks better of it and goes out through the front door and off up the area steps*

The Major comes back from the kitchen with a cup of coffee

Major Here you are ... Oh! That's funny. (*He puts the coffee mug down on the chest, and sees the key, which he picks up. He then opens the drawers and is surprised to find them empty. He goes to the cupboard, looks in and is again surprised to see no clothes. He goes back to the chest and picks up the key again, as ...*)

Jill enters UL

Jill Oh there you are, Alan. I think I ought to do something about finding a hotel for tonight.
Major There's no need. Things have changed. He's gone and he's taken all his stuff with him, and left the key.
Jill Who has? I thought you said the flat was empty tonight.
Major It is now ... I mean now that the plumber's gone and taken all his tools with him, and left the key I gave him.
Jill You mean no-one's going to be sleeping here tonight and I can have my flat back?
Major Yes, I'm happy to say you can. And to celebrate, why don't I take you out to dinner.
Jill I said it was going to be my shout.
Major No, no I won't hear of it. I've had a little windfall.
Jill Sounds as though your horse came in.
Major I wouldn't describe him as a horse, more of a pompous ass.
Jill If you say so. What are we waiting for.
Major Just get my jacket. (*He goes and takes his jacket off the peg from behind the door* UL) Right off we go.
Jill I am looking forward to it.

They go out of the front door and up the area steps, as . . .

Elizabeth and Humphrey come in UL. *Humphrey is carrying a small overnight case*

Elizabeth Anything you want, Humphrey, just give me a shout. You know I'm only upstairs.

Humphrey I've had dinner, but I wouldn't say no to a couple of eggs for breakfast.

Elizabeth I'll bring some down for you.

Humphrey Thank you. Pop them in the kitchen. I'm going to have a bath and turn in early. Had a tiring day.

Elizabeth Of course, you know where everything is, don't you.

Humphrey Don't worry. I'll make myself at home. I'm very adaptable.

Elizabeth I'll leave you then.

Humphrey Thank you. Good-night Elizabeth.

Elizabeth Good-night.

She goes out UL

Humphrey puts his case on the bed and takes out flowered pyjamas and a silk dressing-gown. He closes the case and puts it down, upstage of the bed, so that it cannot be seen. He goes to the phone and dials a number. After a moment he inserts a coin

Humphrey Lorraine's Agency? Humphrey Bennett here. . . . Yes I know you've got a booking for me tomorrow night, but I want one for tonight as well. . . . Yes, as soon as possible. I want an early night.

He puts the receiver down, takes the pyjamas and dressing-gown and goes with them into the bathroom, shutting the door behind him

Philip and Brenda come in through the front door

Brenda I don't know what's happened to Daddy. I suppose he must have gone home. We'll have to see him in the morning.

Philip I'm not looking forward to that. Still he may have calmed down a bit by then.

Brenda I'm sure we'll all feel better after a night's sleep.

Philip I don't think we'll get much sleep.

Brenda Philip!

Philip I mean it's only a single bed.

Brenda I'm sure we'll manage.

Philip I'm ravenous, aren't you?

Brenda Starving. Have you got any food in?

Philip I think I've got a few eggs.

Brenda Shall I make us an omelette?

Philip Lovely.

They go into the kitchen

As the door closes, the bathroom door opens and Humphrey comes out wearing his dressing-gown and carrying his black jacket and pinstripes, which he puts on the bed. He gets his wash-bag out of his suitcase, leaves the case on the bed, and goes to the bathroom, shutting the door

The Major comes in through the front door

The telephone starts to ring. Immediately the Major picks up the receiver

Major Hallo. Hallo. . . . Lorraine's Escort Agency? . . . Captain Chelmsford-Smythe? . . . No I'm afraid he's not . . . Certainly I'll give him the message. "When the account is paid we'll deliver the goods." Don't worry, I'll make sure he gets it. Goodbye. (*He puts the receiver down and looks round the room for his money. He sees the clothes on the bed and is horror-struck. He looks about him. He hears the sounds of running water from the bathroom. He quickly goes to the bathroom door and knocks on it apprehensively*) Mr Clarke?

The running water stops. The door is opened by Humphrey

Humphrey What? Oh it's you.
Major What are you doing here?
Humphrey Using the bathroom, what do you think?
Major But you're not coming till tomorrow.
Humphrey It was Elizabeth's idea. She said I could move in tonight. So I did. (*Pointedly*) So good-night.
Major (*weakly*) Oh, good-night.

Humphrey goes back in the bathroom and shuts the door in the Major's face

There is a noise from the kitchen

Philip (*off*) Oh blast.
Brenda (*off*) Never mind.

The Major in a moment of panic picks up the clothes and the suitcase and runs off UL, shutting the door behind him

Philip and Brenda come out of the kitchen

Philip Somebody's been messing about in my kitchen. I could have sworn I had half a dozen eggs this morning.
Brenda Never mind. Is there anywhere open round here?
Philip Yes. There's an Indian grocer round the corner. They stay open until ten.
Brenda We've just got time.
Philip Come on.

They go out of the front door and up the area steps

The Major comes on UL and just sees them disappearing up the area steps. He opens the chest of drawers and sees that they are empty. He hurries to the cupboard and goes in to look around. The moment he is inside . . .

Elizabeth enters UL. She is carrying a box of eggs, which she takes immediately into the kitchen

The Major comes out of the cupboard and shuts the door behind him

Elizabeth bangs a cabinet door shut in the kitchen. The Major looks at the kitchen, looks to the front door and back to the kitchen

Major My God, he's back! (*He goes to the kitchen and knocks on the door*) Mr Clarke?

The door opens and Elizabeth pops out

Elizabeth Alan?
Major Elizabeth!
Elizabeth Have you been messing about in the kitchen? I left it tidy.
Major Yes. I was just going to cook something for Humphrey. I thought he might be hungry.
Elizabeth He's not. He's had his dinner.
Major He didn't tell me that.
Elizabeth He probably didn't think it was any of your business. Now I suppose I'll have to tidy it all up again.

She goes into the kitchen and shuts the door behind her

The Major dithers, not knowing what to do

We see Jacqueline coming down the area steps. She knocks on the door

The Major reacts, and rushes to answer the door. Jacqueline enters. She is tall, sophisticated and attractive. She has a fur wrap and carries a small valise

Jacqueline Hi. I'm Jacqueline.
Major What do you want?
Jacqueline We'll discuss money later.
Major What for?
Jacqueline Depends on what you want. Let's have a drink and talk about it.
Major I don't want to talk about it.
Jacqueline You want to get on with it straight away, do you? (*She takes her fur wrap off and throws it on the bed, then turns her back on him. Indicating her zip*) Would you mind.
Major What?!! You can't . . . I mustn't . . . You don't understand. My ex-wife's in the kitchen.
Jacqueline Oh I see. You want a threesome do you? That's all right, you're paying.
Major No, no. I don't want that. Quick, get in there. I'll explain later. (*He takes her to the cupboard and opens the door*)
Jacqueline You don't have to explain. I know all about hide-and-seek.

She goes into the cupboard with her valise

The Major sees the fur on the bed and throws it in after her and shuts the door, as . . .

Elizabeth comes out of the kitchen

Elizabeth What are you doing?

Major Just popping something in the cupboard.
Elizabeth Something of Humphrey's?
Major I hadn't thought of that. That would explain it.
Elizabeth Explain what?
Major Why I was popping it in the cupboard.

Humphrey, now in his pyjamas and dressing-gown, comes out of the bathroom, carrying the rest of his clothes

Humphrey Oh! Something wrong?
Elizabeth No. I've put your eggs in the kitchen.
Humphrey Thank you. I'm just going to make myself a cup of tea, before I go to bed. I need an *undisturbed* night's sleep. (*He puts his things on the bed*)
Elizabeth Of course, Humphrey. Good-night.
Humphrey Good-night.

He goes into the kitchen and shuts the door

Elizabeth Come along, Alan.
Major Yes. I'll just put his things away for him.
Elizabeth Don't hang about. He doesn't want to be disturbed.

She goes out UL *leaving the door open*

The Major collects Humphrey's things from the bed, takes them off UL *and returns, shutting the door behind him. He goes towards the cupboard as . . .*

Jill comes down the area steps

He is about to open the cupboard door, when Jill enters

Jill So there you are.
Major Ah! Jill! I hope you've ordered.
Jill No I haven't. You take me to a restaurant, sit me down and suddenly run out without a word. I was stuck there with everybody staring at me. I felt a complete fool.
Major I couldn't find my money.
Jill If you didn't want to go out, you shouldn't have suggested it in the first place.
Major I do want to go out, but just at the moment I can't. I've got something on my mind.
Jill That's all right, we'll forget about it. Now if you'll find my case, I'd like to go to bed.
Major Your case? It must be with all the others.
Jill What others?
Major All the others of your clothes. I'll get it while you go in the bathroom.
Jill Yes I will when you get my case.
Major Right, I'll get it.

He goes out of the door UL

Jill takes off her coat and goes to the cupboard to hang it up

   The Major comes in with her case

   No!

But Jill opens the door and steps back in surprise

Jill What the . . . ?!!

   Jacqueline comes out, now dressed in outrageously sexy gear

Jacqueline Hi. I'm Jacqueline. You must be his ex-wife.

Jill (*to Alan*) So that's why you stood me up. I can see exactly what you'd got on your mind.

Major I don't know what she wants.

Jill Don't worry, *she* knows what *you* want, and so do *I*. (*She goes to the door* UL *and holds it open*) Good-night.

Jacqueline I suppose this is all part of the game, is it? (*Going* UL) Is she going to spank you afterwards.

Jill No, but I'll probably wring his neck.

Jacqueline It's all the same to me.

   She goes out UL

Major But Jill you don't——

Jill No *I* don't, but you apparently *do*. Good-night.

   The Major, helpless, goes out UL

Jill shuts the door and puts the catch on. She then picks up her case, puts it on the bed, takes out her nightie, dressing-gown, slippers and wash-bag and goes into the bathroom, shutting the door

The Major and Jacqueline come down the area steps. The Major peeps through the window and, satisfied that the coast is clear, opens the front door. They enter

Major Quick, get your things and go at once.

Jacqueline All right, please yourself. As long as I get my money, what do I care? So if you'd like to settle up . . . ?

Major Oh . . . um . . . will you take a cheque?

Jacqueline Sorry, cash on the nail.

Major Well, you see, I'm not the one. The person you want isn't here at the moment.

Jacqueline It isn't you then. You mean you're not Mr Bennett? What's going on?

Major It's all a mistake. You see when you came here, he wasn't here, at least I didn't think he was, but he was all the time, although I didn't know it. If I had've done, I would have known then what I didn't know before and I would have known not to put you in the cupboard. Get in the cupboard and get your things.

Jacqueline I've played some funny games in my time, but this beats the lot. I'll have to change before I go.

Major Well go in there and do it.
Jacqueline Yes, all right.

She goes into the cupboard

He shuts the door, tip-toes quickly to the kitchen door and listens, then to the bathroom door. He hears noises inside, runs to the cupboard and opens the door. He reacts

Major Oh my God!
Jacqueline (*off*) Changed your mind?

The Major claps his hand over his eyes and goes in, shutting the door as ...

Jill, now in her nightie and dressing-gown, comes out of the bathroom, carrying her clothes. She puts them on the bed and goes into the kitchen

As she shuts the door, the Major staggers out of the cupboard, his clothes awry, shirt-tail hanging out. He sees ...

Philip and Brenda coming down the area steps

He grabs Jill's things off the bed and goes back into the cupboard. He does not realize he has failed to pick up Jill's bra

Philip and Brenda enter through the front door. Brenda carries a carrier bag of groceries

Brenda I'll get started on our omelettes. (*She goes towards the kitchen door*)
Philip I'm going to have a bit of a wash, I feel grubby.

Brenda stops with her hand on the kitchen door knob

Brenda Tell you what, why don't we get ready for bed before we eat. Be more romantic.
Philip Yes, good idea. (*He goes towards the cupboard*) I hope he's brought my clothes back.
Brenda (*looking round*) Where's my case gone? (*She puts the carrier bag down*)
Philip That fool of a Major's moved it I expect. He just can't leave anything alone. I bet he's stuffed it in the cupboard. (*He has his hand on the cupboard door knob, about to open it*)

Brenda picks up Jill's bra from the bed

Brenda Is that your bra?
Philip What? What are you talking about?
Brenda (*frostily*) It's not mine, and if it's not yours whose is it?
Philip How the hell should I know. It's probably the Major's. He's always getting things mixed up at the cleaners. Ah! Now I know where our clothes are.

Philip goes out UL

Good God, there's a cupboard out here like a clothes shop.

He enters with Brenda's case, which he hands to her, then goes out again

Brenda At least you've got them back.

Philip enters with his pyjamas

Philip I'll sort the rest out in the morning. I don't know what he's up to, but there's something very fishy about all this.

Brenda Don't let's worry about that now, let's get undressed. (*She goes towards the bathroom*) I fancy a shower.

She goes in

Philip Mm, so do I.

He goes into the bathroom and shuts the door

Ronald enters UL *and shuts the door. He carries a bottle of Scotch. He looks out of the window, then looks at his watch*

Ronald Funny. She's late. Very late. (*He takes out a cheque from his pocket, looks at it, smiling broadly, kisses it and puts it back in his pocket. He sprawls on the bed, takes a large cigar out of his pocket and lights it. He puts the bottle on the bedside table*)

Jill enters from the kitchen

Ah, there you are. All ready for bed I see.

Jill Who the devil are you?

Ronald I'm the one they sent you for. Call me Ronnie.

Jill I'll call you something if you don't get out of here at once.

Ronald (*sitting up*) That's a bit strong, we haven't done anything yet.

Jill And we're not going to either. Are you going or do I have to call for help? (*She goes to the door* UL *and opens it*)

Ronald What? (*He gets up off the bed*) Steady on, there's no need to be like that. Aren't you from the Escort Agency?

Jill Certainly not. I'm the ten ... I'm the Major's niece.

Ronald Good Lord, frightfully sorry. My mistake. Got my wires crossed. Not a word to Elizabeth. She might get the wrong end of the stick.

Jill Will you kindly leave?

Ronald Yes of course. Sorry. Just going.

He quickly goes out UL. *Jill shuts the door and puts the catch down. She takes off her dressing-gown and gets into bed. She pulls the hanging switch above the bed and the main room lights go off. She lies down and puts her hand on the bedside lamp switch as ...*

Philip comes out of the bathroom and goes into the kitchen, taking the bag of groceries with him

Jill sits up in bed, astonished. She switches on the main lights and gets out of bed. She puts on her dressing-gown, goes towards the kitchen

The Major backs out of the cupboard, his clothes are very dishevelled

Major Please, leave me alone!

Jill turns and sees him

Jill Major!

Major Ah! (*He quickly shuts the cupboard door*) There's a mouse in there. It's been attacking me.

Jill Oh! Don't let it out. I'm petrified of mice.

Major I'm not letting that mouse from in there out here. It's far too playful.

Jill What are you doing back here? I thought I told you to go.

Major You must let me explain. You see Elizabeth let the flat tonight to Humphrey Bennett QC. That was why I left you at the restaurant, although I didn't want to. I was trying to sort things out.

Jill Why didn't you say so?

Major There wasn't time and there's even less time now. You'll have to sleep in my room upstairs and I'll sleep on the floor.

Jill Well that's simple enough. What's the problem?

Major I can't begin to tell you now. It's full of complications.

Brenda, in her nightie, comes out of the bathroom

Brenda Oh!

Major No time to explain. Your father's here.

Brenda Daddy?

Major He's in the kitchen.

Brenda Where's Philip?

Major (*pointing to the bathroom door*) Can't be there. (*He points to the kitchen door*) Can't be there, certainly not in there ... (*Pointing to the cupboard door*) He must be upstairs. (*He points to the door* UL)

Brenda I must find him and warn him.

Major Not to see your father?

Brenda No. Not to punch him.

She runs off UL

Jill What's she doing here?

Major I'll explain upstairs. Get your things.

Jill I don't know where they are.

Major I do, come on.

Jill Oh, my toothbrush.

She runs into the bathroom

Humphrey enters UL

Humphrey You again!

Major You were in the kitchen!

Humphrey No, upstairs, trying to get a kettle. Damn thing didn't work. Wouldn't believe it, they haven't got a spare one.

Major You didn't see anyone upstairs did you?

Humphrey Course I did. I saw Elizabeth.

Jill comes out of the bathroom with her toothbrush

Ah, there you are my dear. At last. (*To the Major*) We seem to have the same tastes, old boy.

Major No, she's not yours. She's mine.

Jill Yes, I'm his niece.

Major We're just going.

Humphrey I should think so. Shouldn't have been here in the first place. Where's mine then?

Major Oh . . . she must be around here somewhere. Come on, Jill.

The go out UL

Humphrey goes into the bathroom and shuts the door

Jacqueline comes out of the cupboard, dressed in her kinky gear, looks round, then gets into bed and lies down

Ronald looks in through the window, then quickly opens the front door and comes in

Jacqueline (*half-sitting up*) Hi!

Ronald Oh! Hi! Are you from the Agency?

Jacqueline That's right.

Ronald About time too. I was expecting you ages ago. (*He takes his jacket off*)

Jacqueline I'm glad somebody's pleased to see me. I was beginning to think I'd come to the wrong place.

Ronald You're in the right place all right, and I'll join you there. (*He takes off his trousers*)

Jacqueline This is better than hiding in cupboards. I don't really like those sort of games.

Ronald What sort of games do you like? (*He gets into bed*)

Jacqueline Anything you fancy. You're paying.

Ronald In that case, let's give it a whirl.

They lie down

Elizabeth, in her nightclothes, enters UL. *She doesn't see them and goes towards the kitchen*

Ronald Oh I say, this is going to be worth every penny.

Elizabeth Ronald!

Ronald Oh my God, Elizabeth!

He springs out of bed and rushes out UL

Elizabeth Ronald. Come back here, I'll murder you!

She runs out after him

Jacqueline looks resigned, and lies down, covering herself with the duvet

Philip comes out of the kitchen, sees a body in the bed, assumes it is Brenda

Philip Oh there you are, darling. Well, who needs omelettes at a time like this. (*He gets into bed with Jacqueline and snuggles down*) Ooh! Brenda! Oh! Brenda! Ooh!

The Major dashes in UL *and goes towards the kitchen*

Ooh! Brenda, you've changed!
Major I'm not surprised, that's not Brenda.
Philip (*sitting up in bed*) What?!

Jacqueline sits up in bed

Jacqueline Hi! I'm Jacqueline. But you can call me anything you like. Even Brenda.
Major I wouldn't do that if I were you, she's just coming down the stairs.

Philip pushes Jacqueline down

Philip Get down quick. (*He covers her face with the duvet*)

Brenda enters UL

Brenda Philip! What are you doing?
Philip I thought I was doing it with you, Brenda. Ooh!
Brenda What's the matter? Why are you wriggling about?
Philip I'm being goosed! By the goose feathers, in the duvet.
Brenda You can't stay there. Daddy's here.
Philip Daddy! He mustn't find me like this.
Major No he mustn't. Get out of bed and get dressed.
Philip I can't.
Brenda Why not?
Major Yes, why not?
Philip You know!
Major I know, (*to Brenda*) you go in the cupboard.
Brenda What on earth for?
Major To get dressed. Your father won't find you in there. I'll get your clothes. Quick, there's not a moment to lose. (*He ushers Brenda into the cupboard*)

Brenda goes into the cupboard

As soon as she is in, Philip leaps out of bed

Philip She's like an octopus, her hands are everywhere.
Major I know. I had some in the cupboard. In you go.

Philip goes into the cupboard

The Major shuts the door and runs out UL

Humphrey comes out of the bathroom and sees Jacqueline in the bed

Humphrey Ah, there you are at long last. You *are* from the Agency aren't you?
Jacqueline Of course I am. Do I look as if I'm from the Salvation Army?
Humphrey I'll say you don't. (*He takes off his dressing-gown and gets into bed*)

The Major runs in UL *followed by Jill*

Major No time for that. Brenda's here.
Humphrey What? Brenda *here*? (*He leaps out of bed*)
Major And Philip. He'll be a witness for the prosecution.
Jacqueline Who's Brenda? Your wife?
Jill Worse than that. His daughter.
Major (*to Humphrey*) In the bathroom. I'll get your clothes.

Humphrey dashes into the bathroom

Ronald runs in UL

Ronald She's going to murder me.

He runs off into the kitchen

Major (*to Jacqueline*) Quick, under the bed.

Jacqueline gets under the bed on the upstage side

(*To Jill*) You, in the bed.

Jill gets into bed

Jill And you?
Major Excuse me. In for a penny, in for pound.

He gets into bed next to her. She lies down. He covers her with the duvet as . . .

Elizabeth, brandishing a riding crop, enters UL

Elizabeth Where is he? I'll kill him. (*She sees the Major*) What are you doing in Humphrey's bed?
Major Nothing. I'm just having a little rest before I go to bed.

He pulls the duvet up, revealing Jill's feet. Elizabeth looks at them in surprise

Elizabeth What are you doing painting your toe-nails?

The Major looks at them in horror

Major Er . . . those aren't my feet . . . I mean they're not my feet as you normally see them. I got involved with some amateur theatricals . . . an ex-servicemen's group . . . all men . . . so they made me play a woman. And once I'd got it on, I couldn't get it off.
Elizabeth You'll tell me next your legs are five feet long.
Major I think they must have grown a bit.

The feet slowly withdraw

But they're shrinking again now.
Elizabeth Nonsense! You've got somebody in there.
Major No I haven't. (*He wriggles about in the bed*)
Elizabeth Then what are you wriggling for?
Major I've got an itch.
Elizabeth I'll scratch it for you.
Major No!

Elizabeth pulls back the duvet, and Jill sits up

Elizabeth You! What are you doing in bed with your uncle?
Jill He's not my uncle.
Major No I'm not, we're just good friends.
Jill Yes, *very* good friends. We're married.
Elizabeth ⎱ (*together*) What?!!
Major   ⎰
Elizabeth (*to the Major*) Why didn't you tell me before?
Major I didn't know before, because we weren't married before.
Elizabeth Before what? When did you get married?
Major When did we get married?
Jill Today. We were going to keep it a secret.

There is a loud sneeze from Jacqueline under the bed

Elizabeth What was that?
Major That's another secret we were going to keep.
Elizabeth There's somebody under the bed. Come out of there whoever you are.

Jacqueline appears from under the bed

  Another of your wives?
Major No she's not the bride, she's the bridesmaid.
Elizabeth She looks like a cheap tart to me.
Jacqueline That's one thing I'm not. I'm not cheap.
Elizabeth (*to the Major*) I caught Ronnie in bed with her.
Major Yes, poor girl, she's had a lot to put up with.
Elizabeth (*to Jacqueline*) What were you doing in that bed with my husband?
Jacqueline Well we weren't reading a book at bedtime.
Major You know what weddings are like, they put ideas into people's heads.
Elizabeth It doesn't take a wedding to put that sort of idea into Ronnie's head. What's she doing here anyway?
Major You see. She had nowhere to stay, so she's joined us on our honeymoon.
Elizabeth In this flat? But I've let it to *Humphrey*.

Humphrey enters from the bathroom

Humphrey Did somebody call?
Elizabeth Humphrey! What *is* going on with these girls in your flat?
Humphrey I deny everything. I've never seen either of them before.
Major No, I don't think you've met my wife.
Humphrey Of course I've met Elizabeth.
Major No, not Elizabeth. This wife.
Humphrey You mean you've left Elizabeth already.
Major No, she left me.
Elizabeth We're divorced.

Humphrey That didn't last long, did it! Hard lines, Chelmsford-Smythe.
Elizabeth Chelmsford-Smythe? That's my husband.
Humphrey You mean your *ex*-husband.
Elizabeth He will be when I catch up with him. He's got some girl called
  Brenda pregnant.
Humphrey What?! (*To the Major*) So it wasn't Philip, it was *you*! How dare
  you make my daughter pregnant.
Jill Did you make his daughter pregnant?
Major Well, in a roundabout sort of way, but it was all a mistake.
Humphrey Yes I should say it was. You should be ashamed of yourself at
  your age.
Jill As far as I'm concerned our marriage is off.
Major But you don't understand. I don't even know Brenda. I'll prove it.
  (*He goes to the cupboard and opens the door*) Brenda, come out here and
  tell your father I didn't make you pregnant.

Brenda comes out of the cupboard

Brenda Daddy, what are you doing here?
Elizabeth Your father rented this flat from me.
Humphrey Never mind about me, what were you doing in that cupboard?
Brenda (*pointing to the Major*) I was waiting for him to give me my clothes.
Humphrey So he *has* made you pregnant. You've been at it in the cupboard
  with him. (*He points to the Major*)
Brenda No, not him, Philip.

Philip comes out of the cupboard

Humphrey You've been at it with him as well?
Philip Good-evening, Mr Bennett.
Jacqueline Mr Bennett? (*She goes to him*) Why didn't you say so before?
  You're running into overtime now.
Brenda Daddy, you're not up to naughties again are you?
Humphrey What? Er ... has anybody met my secretary? No? This is my
  secretary.
Major Brenda, I think you should tell your father the truth. I am not the
  father of your baby.
Brenda Of course you're not.
Jill (*pleased*) Alan you're not?
Humphrey Then who is?
Major (*pointing to Philip*) He is.
Philip Brenda, why didn't you tell me?
Brenda Because I'm not.
Humphrey (*to Philip*) You swine. I'll kill you.
Major Careful, Humphrey, your "secretary" might be taking notes.
Jacqueline Yes I never take cheques, only notes.
Humphrey What? Oh, yes, quite. (*To Philip*) I presume you have marriage
  in mind?
Philip Well I would, but I haven't got a job.
Humphrey No, and you're not likely to get one either.

Major Humphrey, has your wife met your new secretary?

Brenda I'm sure Mummy would be fascinated to meet her.

Humphrey Philip, my dear fellow, very sorry about that little misunderstanding this morning. Glad to have you back in chambers.

Philip Thanks, Dad.

Humphrey winces

Major Well done, Grandpa!

Humphrey goes to speak, thinks better of it

Elizabeth I can't understand for the life of me what all these people are doing in my basement flat.

Philip It's not yours. You may think you're the Mother Superior, but you're only the cleaning lady.

Elizabeth How dare you!

Major I think there's been some misunderstanding.

Philip No there hasn't. You told me

Major Yes I told you never to be caught in bed with another man's "secretary". Remember, I did you a favour.

Philip Yes, I'm afraid I do remember.

Elizabeth You're talking in riddles. (*To the Major*) What are they all doing here?

Major We're having a little party to celebrate our marriage. That's why Ronnie was in here. I asked him to join us.

Elizabeth Ronnie!

Ronald comes out of the kitchen

Ronald Yes, my dear?

Elizabeth What were you doing in bed with Humphrey's secretary at Alan's wedding party, and where are your trousers?

Ronald I refuse to say anything until I've taken legal advice.

Humphrey If you want Counsel's opinion and you want to plead *calumniae litium* I should say *incognita cause* . . . you're up the creek.

Elizabeth And who is this Brenda you've got pregnant?

Humphrey What?! You got my daughter pregnant?

Brenda But Daddy, I'm not pregnant.

Humphrey You're very lucky the way you're leaping from bed to bed.

Ronald What's all this about Alan's wedding party?

Major I'm having a little celebration. (*Indicating Jill*) This is my wife.

Ronald Good gracious. I thought she was your "niece".

Major Certainly not, what sort of an uncle do you think I am?

Jill (*to Elizabeth*) I thought you were married to him. (*She points to Philip*)

Elizabeth The plumber?

Philip What are you talking about? I don't know the first thing about plumbing.

Elizabeth That's why my husband fired you.

Brenda Philip, I didn't know you were a plumber as well.

Philip Don't believe a word she says. She's a struck-off nun.

Elizabeth What!

Philip (*pointing to the Major*) That's what he told me. You said she lived in the attic.

Humphrey (*to Elizabeth*) He told me he was married to you. He was Chelmsford-Smythe, the adjutant.

Ronald I'm Chelmsford-Smythe, the adjutant. He said his wife was his niece.

Jill (*to Philip*) He said you were the adjutant.

Elizabeth No, no, he said he was the plumber.

Brenda He told everybody I was pregnant.

Major I do seem to have said rather a lot, don't I.

Jacqueline He didn't say anything to me.

Major I know when to keep my mouth shut.

Elizabeth Alan, I demand an explanation. What's been going on in my house?

Major Well ... !

Ronald It's not your house.

Elizabeth What?

Ronald The General's will, remember? The codicil. If Alan remarried he was to get the house.

Major I thought he hated me.

Ronald Not half has much as he hated me.

Major Elizabeth, is this true?

Elizabeth It was a condition of the will. You weren't to be told until you remarried.

Major Well I'm blessed.

Jill I bet you're glad I "married" you.

Major It'll be nice being married.

Elizabeth Ronald, we're homeless, what are we going to do?

Major Don't worry you can rent the flat from me. I'm good at letting flats.

Elizabeth But we've got no money.

Ronald That's all you know. I put three hundred quid on a forecast at the dogs, and it came up at fify to one. (*He takes the cheque out of his pocket*) Here you are, certified cheque for fifteen thousand pounds.

Elizabeth Where did you get the three hundred pounds from?

Ronald I came across it in Alan's pocket. Just a loan, old boy!

Major The rent money. That was Humphrey's rent money.

Elizabeth *My* rent money. Oh Ronald, you are clever.

Major Not so clever as you think. *My* house, *my* rent money, *my* winnings. Thank you, Ronald. (*He takes the cheque*) You've repaid the loan with interest. Four thousand nine hundred and ninety per cent to be precise. Come on, Jill.

Jill Where are we going?

Major To find a vicar—we've got too much to lose.

They go out UL *as——*

—the CURTAIN *falls*

FURNITURE AND PROPERTY LIST

ACT I

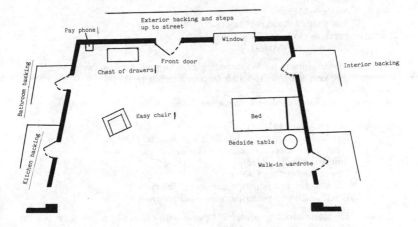

SCENE 1

On stage: Single bed with bedding. *On it:* large teddy bear night-dress case. *Under pillow:* night-dress
Bedside table. *On it:* bedside lamp
Chest of drawers. *On it:* toiletries, hair lacquer, etc. *In drawers:* **Jill's** clothes
Small easy chair. *On it:* small suitcase, car keys, handbag
Pay-phone on wall
Window curtains (open)
Carpet
In walk-in cupboard: **Jill's** clothes on hangers, evening bag
Hook on door UL

Off stage: Empty milk bottle **(Jill)**
Letters **(Major)**
Bottle of milk, car keys **(Jill)**
Philip's clothes on hangers **(Major)**
Jill's clothes on hangers **(Major)**
Teddy bear **(Major)**
Mug of coffee **(Jill)**
Key **(Major)**

Key, empty pink dustbin bag, blue dustbin bag containing pair of boxing
   gloves, men's toiletries, etc. **(Major)**
Duvet, pillow, pyjamas **(Major)**
3 chest of drawers with **Philip's** clothes **(Major)**
Philip's clothes **(Major)**
Key, small valise **(Philip)**
Plastic bag of groceries, handbag with car keys **(Jill)**
Philip's jacket **(Jill)**
Philip's trousers with 10p coins in pocket **(Major)**
2 of **Jill's** drawers with **Jill's** clothes from cupboard on top **(Major)**
Dressing-gown **(Philip)**
Jill's 3rd drawer **(Major)**
Case **(Jill)**
Négligé **(Major)**
3 of **Philip's** drawers **(Major)**
Previous clothes **(Jill)**
Jill's drawers **(Major)**

Personal: **Major:** coins in pocket including £1 coin and 10p coin, wrist-watch
            Jill: key, coins, wrist-watch (*required throughout*)

SCENE 2

Off stage: Zoo catalogue **(Major)**
             Key, holdall containing barrister's gown, etc. **(Philip)**
             Pinstripe trousers, black jacket **(Philip)**
             Suitcase, handbag **(Jill)**
             One or two clothes **(Jill)**
             Black jacket and pinstripe trousers **(Major)**
             Black jacket and pinstripe trousers **(Philip)**

Personal: **Elizabeth:** handbag containing purse with coins, £20 note, letter
            Humphrey: wallet with £300

ACT II

Off stage: Philip's 3 drawers **(Major)**
             Jill's clothes **(Jill)**
             Philip's clothes including wig **(Jill)**
             Large bouquet of flowers **(Philip)**
             Philip's clothes **(Major)**
             2 pairs shoes **(Major)**
             Vacuum cleaner—practical **(Elizabeth)**
             Suitcase **(Brenda)**
             Previous clothes **(Philip)**
             Bouquet of flowers **(Major)**
             Philip's clothes **(Major)**
             Cup of coffee **(Major)**
             Small case containing pyjamas, dressing-gown, wash-bag **(Humphrey)**
             Black jacket, pinstripe trousers **(Humphrey)**
             Box of eggs **(Elizabeth)**
             Small valise containing sexy gear **(Jacqueline)**
             Shirt, etc. **(Humphrey)**

Jill's case containing night-dress, dressing-gown, slippers, wash-bag
(**Major**)
Clothes (**Jill**)
Bag of groceries (**Brenda**)
Brenda's case (**Philip**)
Pyjamas (**Philip**)
Bottle of Scotch (**Ronald**)
Toothbrush (**Jill**)
Riding crop (**Elizabeth**)

Personal: **Major:** pen, £300 in pocket, wrist-watch
Elizabeth: coins, key with label
Ronald: address book, coins, cheque, wrist-watch, cigar, lighter
Humphrey: coins

LIGHTING PLOT

Practical fittings required: main lights (with hanging switch above bed), bedside light, lights in kitchen and bathroom, off

ACT I, SCENE 1   Morning

To open: General interior lighting

Cue 1	**Philip** goes into the bathroom and switches on the light *Snap up bathroom light*	(Page 10)
Cue 2	**Jill** switches off main electricity switch *Snap off light in bathroom*	(Page 11)
Cue 3	**Major** switches on main electricity switch *Snap up light in bathroom*	(Page 12)

ACT I, SCENE 2   Late afternoon

To open: General interior lighting

Cue 4	**Elizabeth** switches on main lights *Snap up main lights*	(Page 23)
Cue 5	**Elizabeth** switches on bathroom light *Snap up bathroom light*	(Page 26)
Cue 6	**Elizabeth** switches on kitchen light *Snap up kitchen light*	(Page 26)

ACT II,   Evening

To open: Main lights on, kitchen and bathroom lights on

Cue 7	**Jill** pulls hanging switch above bed *Snap off main lights*	(Page 60)
Cue 8	**Jill** switches on main lights *Snap up main lights*	(Page 60)

EFFECTS PLOT

ACT I

Cue 1   **Major** enters UL   (Page 1)
         Doorbell rings

Cue 2   **Major:** "... I would, would you?"   (Page 3)
         Kettle whistles off in kitchen

Cue 3   **Jill** goes into kitchen   (Page 3)
         Cut kettle noise

Cue 4   **Jill** goes up area steps   (Page 6)
         Pause, then car door opens and slams, engine starts

Cue 5   **Jill** grabs her handbag from the bed   (Page 6)
         Telephone rings

Cue 6   **Jill** goes out of the front door   (Page 7)
         Pause, then car door slams and car drives off

Cue 7   **Major** hangs up man's clothes in cupboard   (Page 7)
         High-powered motor bike approaches

Cue 8   **Major** reappears from bathroom   (Page 7)
         Motor bike stops

Cue 9   **Philip** shuts the bathroom door behind him   (Page 10)
         Car approaches, stops, car door opens and slams

Cue 10   **Jill** hangs her suit in the cupboard   (Page 20)
         Telephone rings

Cue 11   **Elizabeth** pulls out Jill's night-dress   (Page 26)
         Telephone rings

Cue 12   **Major** goes towards cupboard   (Page 32)
         Telephone rings

ACT II

Cue 13   **Philip:** "... her father wouldn't let me."   (Page 40)
         Telephone rings

Cue 14   **Major:** "Er ... Chelmsford-Smythe."   (Page 46)
         Taxi horn honks, off

Cue 15   **Major** comes in front door   (Page 55)
         Telephone rings

Cue 16   As the **Major** looks about him   (Page 55)
           Sound of running water from bathroom

Cue 17   **Major:** "Mr Clarke?"   (Page 55)
           Running water stops

Cue 18   **Jill** goes into bathroom   (Page 58)
           Water etc. noises from bathroom

Cue 19   **Major:** "Oh my God!"   (Page 59)
           Cut bathroom noises

MADE AND PRINTED IN GREAT BRITAIN BY
LATIMER TREND & COMPANY LTD PLYMOUTH
MADE IN ENGLAND